SILENT VICTIM

SILENT VICTIM

GROWING UP IN A CHILD PORN RING

TIMMY FIELDING

iUniverse, Inc.
Bloomington

Silent Victim
Growing Up in a Child Porn Ring

iUniverse books may be ordered through booksellers or by contacting:

iUniverse
1663 Liberty Drive
Bloomington, IN 47403
www.iuniverse.com
1-800-Authors (1-800-288-4677)

ISBN: 978-1-4697-5828-2 (sc)
ISBN: 978-1-4697-5830-5 (hc)
ISBN: 978-1-4697-5829-9 (e)

Library of Congress Control Number: 2012901656

Printed in the United States of America

iUniverse rev. date: 2/24/2012

CONTENTS

CHAPTER ONE

OUR SECRET

I woke up and quietly dressed for another day of survival.

Tommy, my older brother, opened my bedroom door and said, "Hurry, Timmy. Let's go before Mom wakes up."

Tom was eleven—two years older than I was—and had blond hair combed to the side, intense blue eyes, and a slender, athletic build. I was already in silent mode; no one had to tell me. Even at our age, we knew waking up Mom was a very bad idea. Mom wasn't very tall, but she was overweight. She had black hair, wore lots of makeup, and dressed to impress others. She had a smile that won over adults and a scowl that sent chills down her kids' spines.

I met Tom in the kitchen and he was getting some breakfast. We would try to be out of the house for most of the day, playing with our friends—well, really Tommy's friends, because he was popular. He was outgoing, funny, and quick witted. I was kind of short and slender and shy. I had sandy blond hair too, but my eyes were green. It only took one look to tell we were brothers.

I hurried up and looked back to see if my room was picked up. I had to be very careful because Mom hated a dirty or messy room. I did not want to give her a reason to be mad at me. I grabbed a piece of bread and followed my brother outside and down the street. We headed across an empty field and about another quarter-mile past the railroad tracks to a baseball field. No one was there yet. The other kids most likely didn't have to sneak out of the house at the crack of dawn to avoid their mothers.

Tom and I played catch and I knew it would be the only time I would be playing. Once the other kids showed up and picked teams, there wouldn't be any place left for me. I was used to it; I never got picked for sports. At first, it bothered me that even my own brother wouldn't pick me. But they were older and bigger and I sucked, so I probably wouldn't have picked me either. I got to be the scorekeeper that they didn't really need. But most of the time, I would just daydream. Tom's friends arrived and they played baseball until about noon, or just until they got bored. A football game was next on their agenda, which didn't matter to me because I still wouldn't get picked. Tom asked me to run home to get the football.

I looked at him terrified and asked, "What about Mom?"

All the other boys were looking at me.

One said, "You're small. You can just sneak in and she'll never see you."

I knew that was bullshit. Every kid there knew how crazy my mom was. Her stories were legendary around our neighborhood. It was no wonder that no one else offered to go with me.

I knew it would be a dangerous mission. I would have to be quiet enough that she wouldn't even know I was there. I took off at a run. About a block from the house, I slowed down to catch my breath and switch into stealth mode.

As I approached the house, I figured I had a better chance going in the back door instead of the front door. I opened the door very slowly and quietly. I listened very carefully to try to figure out where she might be. All was quiet—even the television was off. I snuck down the hall to my room and searched, but the football wasn't there. It had to be in Tommy's room. As quietly as possible, still in stealth mode, I made it to his room. There it was, sitting on his shelf. I grabbed it and quietly went back down the hall.

Just then I heard the toilet flush and the bathroom door opened. There I was face to face with my mom! She looked right at me, her face distorted with anger, and asked, "Why are you sneaking around? And by the way, have you looked at your room lately? It's a pigsty. You better go clean it up right now, or so help me God, you will regret it."

I ran to my room to clean. I never knew how much time to spend in there to satisfy my mother. I thought thirty minutes would do for today. How wrong I was.

My mother caught me in the living room as I was trying to leave. Without even looking at the room, she was already furious. Whoever, or whatever, had made her mad I would never know, but Tom and I would be the ones she took it out on. She grabbed a broomstick that she kept conveniently handy and dragged me by my arm to my room. I pulled against her, trying to get away. She held tight, screaming all the reasons why I needed a beating. "You call this clean? You call this clean? This is a pigsty!" She reached back for a good long swing and I turned away, but she connected with my back. She went from one side to the other, trying to get as much of me as she could. After about ten hits with the broomstick, she walked over to the bed and pulled the covers off and flipped the mattress over. Then she walked over to the dresser and dumped every drawer out all over the floor. The closet was next and that was also emptied out on the floor until there were piles all over my room. I was crying in the corner of the room and praying she would just leave.

"This room better be perfectly cleaned right this time!"

She stormed out. That was my mom. She smoked and drank occasionally and took prescription drugs like they were candy. The worst part was that she was pissed off almost all the time. She could be very violent at those times. She always lectured us about how lucky we were because her father had been a lot worse when she was growing up. Her father was constantly beating her and her sisters. He had broken her nose once—and he did sick things like put bloody chicken heads in their beds. Yeah, we had it easy compared to her. Boy, did we feel lucky.

After I had been cleaning for ten minutes, she opened the door and said, "Look what you've done."

She showed me a scratch on her arm that must have happened while she grabbed me.

"I'm sorry, Mom."

She reached back and slapped me. Since I was covering my face with my hands, she decided she could punch me. The first one hit my stomach and I leaned over to gasp for air. She punched whatever she could reach after that. I started to scream and cry again. She finally stopped and I went back to cleaning my room.

Dad would be home around five o'clock. He was a big guy, about six feet tall with broad shoulders and muscles from working hard. He had a handsome face and mustache, brown hair, and blue eyes. He was a quiet man and worked hard to support our family. When he came home at night, he wanted everyone to get along. He didn't want to be the one to have to solve the problems at home.

Tom finally made it home and told me that instead of playing football, they had all gone to the park to swim. I knew then, that they had sent me to get the football just to get rid of me.

Six o'clock was always dinnertime and all was quiet—so far. Mom was a good cook and always had a nice meal ready for my dad. She would always purposely put plenty of vegetables on my plate because she knew I hated them. Tommy was talking to Dad about how great it was to go swimming and spend the day with his friends. After a while, Mom joined the conversation but I just sat there quietly.

"Ask your son what he's been up to," she said.

I was in shock while she showed her scratch and some bruises she had somehow gotten while hitting me.

Dad yelled, "What did you do? You know your mom is working hard around here. You can't seem to behave yourself. Eat everything on your plate and then go to bed."

With Dad on her side, she jumped up and dumped my food on my head. She said, "That's all you can say to him after all he did to me."

I sat there with food all over my face and hands. It was such a humiliating experience. With tears in my eyes, I asked to be excused. To calm my mom down, my dad offered to take her out. They drove off and the kitchen and the table were a real mess. Since I knew they had better be clean before Mom got home, I did that and went right to bed.

The next morning, Tommy woke me up and we got off to another early start. When we got outside, I said, "You go on and meet your friends. I'm going across the street to play at the school today."

I knew they didn't want me around and I didn't want a repeat of the day before.

Tommy said, "Fine. You know where I'll be if you want me. Just don't go home."

I knew I needed some time alone because I was still really mad at him for what he did to me.

I walked across the street toward the school; even though it was locked, I knew how to get through the fence. There were some good things about being small. I walked all around the building to see what kind of improvements they were doing. I decided to check out my room for the upcoming year.

I was surprised to find the door to the third grade room open. Inside, a tall man with black hair, brown eyes, and a mustache was putting books up. I could tell he was in good shape because his shoulders and arms were a lot bigger than normal people's.

I figured he must work out.

He smiled and asked, "Hey, what's your name?"

Startled, I answered, "I'm—I'm Timmy."

"Well, Timmy, don't just stand there. Give me a hand. Grab those books and start putting them on the shelf. By the way, what are you doing here? Most kids stay as far away from school in the summer as they can. But you're here like you can't get enough of it." He smiled and before I could answer he said, "By the way, I'm Brian Gunther. I teach third grade here. What grade are you going into?"

"I'm going into third."

"Well, Timmy, you've got a 50 percent chance of being in my class this year. You're kind of a quiet kid, Timmy. What's your story?"

"Story? I don't have one. I just can't be at home and my older brother is hanging out with his friends. I didn't have anything to do so I came to play at school."

We worked at putting everything in order for a few more hours. He kept up the conversation, sometimes getting me to open up because he was easy to talk to.

"Where do you live, Timmy?"

"On Madison Road, right across the street."

"Then you don't need a ride home. Thanks for all your help, but I've got to go now."

"Will you be here tomorrow?"

"Yes," he replied, and then we left.

Since I knew I couldn't go home that early, I went to the playground to kill time.

That night, I waited until Dad got home before I went into the house. Everyone seemed to be over last night's— major event and I surely wasn't going to bring it up either. At dinner, Mom and Dad and Tom all talked about their day. I listened and enjoyed not being noticed.

The next morning, Tommy woke me up early again. He was mad at me and I didn't know why. I hated it when he was mad so I went to the kitchen and made us both toast. He just took it and threw it in the trash.

"Tom, you ass!" I said.

At that moment, Mom walked in. She said, "I can't believe the crap coming out of your mouth."

She grabbed my hair—I was surprised there was any left after last time—and I held on as she dragged me to the bathroom. She slammed my face into the sink, busting both my lips open. Then she grabbed the soap and told me how dirty my mouth was. She kept putting it in and out of my mouth until soap and blood were gushing from my mouth. She only stopped when she realized how much blood was in the sink.

I ran out of the house, across the street, and through the fence to school.

The classroom door was closed, because it was still early. So I sat against the wall with my head on my legs and fell asleep. It seemed like I had been there for hours when I heard my name.

"Timmy, Timmy wake up." When I looked up, Mr. Gunther said, "Oh my God, what happened to your face?" I had two fat lips and a bump on my forehead. "Let's clean you up." He washed my face while I told him what had happened. He just listened quietly. "Hey, you need a break. I live on the other side of the school and I have a pool. Let's go swimming today."

"Really? Can we?"

He nodded and off we went.

He had a large house with a pool and a gym in the garage. There were bedrooms that weren't even being used. I could tell that he lived alone. While he went to put on his bathing suit, I looked around at all the family pictures. When he appeared, I said, "Mr. Gunther, I don't have a suit. What will I swim in?"

"Just wear your underwear." I was shocked, and he could tell how uncomfortable I was. "Timmy, we're both guys, it's no big deal."

I undressed and we went into the pool. He jumped in right after me and we played and swam most of the day. He had a way of throwing me where I would do a back flip and land on my feet every time. I loved it. After about ten flips, he was getting tired. I wasn't tired at all—I could have done that all day.

He stopped and turned me around. Pointing to my back and touching my bruises, he asked, "Timmy, what happened?"

When I told him about the other night, he was shocked. He told me I was a beautiful kid and things like that shouldn't happen to me. He was kind and gentle and kept telling me how special I was—and then he kissed me on my forehead. I wasn't used to that much attention or that many compliments, and I didn't know what to think.

When we got out of the pool, he started the barbecue and made us hamburgers. He talked in a way no one had ever talked to me before—like I counted for something. I left that afternoon really feeling good about myself—like I was important.

"Do you want a ride home?"

"No, I don't live far."

"Timmy, will I see you tomorrow?"

"Really? You want me to come tomorrow?"

"Sure. Maybe we'll do something special. Come early." I couldn't wait.

The next morning, I left the house really early, even before my brother woke up. I ran all the way to Mr. Gunther's house. He was ready too, and we got into his car and we were off. "Where are we going?"

"To the beach. This time I brought you a swimsuit."

I laughed and said, "This time I brought my own."

Since the one he had bought was a lot nicer than mine, I wore his. We had a great day playing in the water and he taught me how to ride the waves. After a while, he got tired and went to lie out, but I stayed in the water as long as I could. He called and told me it was time for lunch. He was great! He always made time to tell me how cute and special I was and would kiss me on the forehead and the cheek. I loved spending time with my new friend. After lunch, we walked on the pier and he bought us ice cream. I got home kind of late but still in time for dinner.

For the next couple of weeks, I spent every day with Mr. Gunther. If he had something to do, he just took me with him. I loved it.

One morning, I got to his house early and he was mowing the yard. I wanted to help so I pulled weeds in the flowerbed out in the back by the pool. I knew I wanted to do a great job for him so I pulled every weed I could find. It was so hot that I took my shirt off. He told me how good I looked, and it made me feel really good.

The next thing I knew, he grabbed me and tossed me into the pool. The water felt great, but it also surprised me. He took off all his clothes and jumped in the pool naked. I was shocked but, since he acted like it was no big deal, I did too. We swam and played and he started throwing me so I could do a back flip, my favorite game. "Timmy, I can't throw you with your pants on. Take them off and it will make it easier."

I trusted him completely. I started to take them off, but it was hard because they were wet. He started to help me and the next thing I knew, he was kissing my neck and telling me what a beautiful kid I was. Then he changed and told me he would never hurt me.

That was my first sexual experience with Mr. Gunther. I was so scared and was crying uncontrollably. I was cold and confused, but he told me to calm down. He picked me up and carried my limp body to his bedroom.

On his bed, I cried softly as he started to fix my hair. "Now, Timmy, you know that I love you. Don't you love me?"

I nodded. He started to kiss my face and neck. I was frightened and tightened up again so he stopped.

"Just relax, Timmy."

He reassured me that nothing else would happen. He held me and told me to close my eyes. I was so confused and scared that my mind shut off and I soon fell asleep.

When I woke up a little later, I could smell food. I went down to the kitchen.

"Are you hungry, Timmy?"

I didn't know what to say and just nodded. He laughed and told me how cute I was and said that we were best buddies.

"I'm going to the beach tomorrow. Do you want to go?"

I nodded.

"What happened here today, Timmy, is our secret."

I nodded.

"Friends keep friends' secrets."

I nodded again. Then he acted like nothing had happened—and I did too.

When it was time to go home, I walked slowly because it hurt so much. I tried to figure out who I could talk to about how dirty I felt. I was so confused. I knew I couldn't tell my family. I wasn't even sure of what had happened or how to explain it. Mom would blame me and Dad would make me stay home. Then Mom would have her way with me every day and that wasn't a good thought.

At dinner, I was quiet—and that wasn't normal since I had been bragging about my new friend for weeks. I had told them my friend was my age. I didn't want to tell them he was a teacher because they would think I was a pest and wouldn't let me hang out with him. I told them about swimming—but never about going to the beach or anywhere else.

Mom said, "Why are you so quiet? And why aren't you eating?" I couldn't tell her that I was too upset and the smell of food was making me sick. So I said, "I don't feel very good."

She felt my face and said, "You don't feel warm. You know the rules—everything on your plate must be gone. Start eating."

I just picked at it—and it wasn't long before it was just Mom and me at the table. She grabbed my fork and picked up some broccoli. She said, "Open your mouth."

I did.

"Now chew!"

I chewed as fast as I could. I didn't even have a chance to swallow before she jammed more broccoli into my mouth as I gagged.

"Don't you dare," she yelled. She grabbed some peas and jammed them in next. "Don't you dare!"

It was too late. I threw up all over my plate and the table. She grabbed me by my hair and dragged me to my room, reaching for the broomstick as she went. Her eyes turned as black as her hair as she yelled with every swing. I had to protect my butt because it hurt so much. I took the hits on my arms and back. I had been emotionally crushed because of earlier—and now she made me feel completely defeated. I felt dirty, as if I deserved to be beaten, as I cried myself to sleep that night.

The next day, I convinced myself that the only one who truly loved me was Mr. Gunther. He even said I could call him Brian when we weren't in public.

I found a note from my mom on the kitchen table telling me to finish eating my dinner before I left the house. I picked up the plate and put all the food into a brown bag and left.

When I got to school, I threw the dinner in the trash and walked to Brian's house. Brian was loading up his car for our beach trip. On the way, we talked about everything—except what had happened the day before.

Even though it was crowded, we got a good parking spot near the beach. I had my swim trunks on under my pants and took them off. When I was getting ready to take my shirt off, Brian stopped me.

"What happened to your back? You have bruises all over it. You need to keep your shirt on today."

I said I would. And as we set our towels out on the sand to lie on them, I told him what had happened.

He didn't say much, just took it all in. With tears in his eyes, he told me what a great kid I was and how very special I was to him. His words made me feel really good about myself.

"Timmy, let's go swimming."

We swam for what seemed like a long time. When Brian started to get out of the water, I asked if I could stay in and play longer.

"Not today. Let's take a walk on the pier and get an ice cream."

On the way home, we were both kind of quiet. For the longest time, the radio wasn't even on. I didn't care—I just liked being with him.

When we pulled into the driveway, it was only 2:30, but he said, "You better go home."

"Mr. Gunther, please no—not yet. It's too early!"

"Timmy, you have to. I've got other things I have to do today."

I got out of the car feeling really sad. I thanked him for the day and started walking home slowly. I wasn't sure where I was going, but I knew I wasn't going home.

I got about two blocks from his house, when Brian pulled up beside me and asked, "Hey kid, do you need a ride?"

I smiled and got in.

At his house, he told me to take a shower so I did. I had shampoo in my hair when Brian stepped in. I was shocked but not scared. I had never even seen my own dad naked, but I had seen Brian twice already. He washed my back and kissed my bruises. As he showered, I watched and I noticed he was getting excited. We got out and dried off.

He led me to the bed and leaned me over the side of the mattress. Then he molested me. I didn't even resist—I yelled because it hurt. It didn't hurt as badly as it had the first time. When he was done, he rolled me over and tickled me. That's when he finally got me to laugh.

Afterward, he told me that next week when school started I would be in his class. I told him how much trouble I usually had in school and that I didn't have very many friends.

He just smiled and said, "Not this year, Timmy. You are in my class and you're going to do great. I promise. And tomorrow, I'm going to buy you some clothes. I am tired of you looking like shit."

We went to Sears, JC Penney, and Kmart, and then went out to eat. On the way home, we even stopped to play miniature golf. What a great day it was for me. He was constantly building me up and giving me compliments.

When we got back to his house, I asked how we would explain all the new clothes to my parents. He told me that we would take the tags off and wash them and tell them that my friend had given me his brother's hand-me-downs.

CHAPTER TWO

THE FIRST DAY OF SCHOOL

Mom always took us on the first day of school so she could meet our teachers and act like she really cared about us. It never impressed our teachers because they could always see through it—and then they would feel sorry for us.

But this day would be different. I wasn't afraid to go to school. I put on my new clothes and Mom scrambled us some eggs and off we went to school. While we walked to school, my brother was begging her not to meet his teacher. He said he was too old for that, but it didn't deter my mom—she enjoyed his humiliation. Finally, she slapped his face and asked, "You embarrassed of your mother?"

He answered appropriately, knowing there was no winning this battle.

I wanted Mom to meet Mr. Gunther. I didn't know why, I just did. I knew she would make me look bad and Mr. Gunther wouldn't like her. When we got to the door, she looked inside and gasped.

"Boy is he cute."

Brian had on a dark blue button-down shirt and pleated khaki pants and every hair was in place. He kind of looked like a model. Then she fixed her hair and went in. I was surprised at how nice she was.

She said, "Hi, my name is Linda Fielding." She put her arm around me and told Mr. Gunther how special I was. Boy was I shocked! She also told him I wasn't that bright and I had even been held back a year. That sounded more like my mom.

Mr. Gunther smiled and said, "I have a feeling this will be a good year for Timmy."

"I sure hope so," she said before excusing herself.

To my surprise Mr. Gunther introduced me to the class and put my desk next to his in front of the class. He told them I was his assistant.

The class stared at me and I smiled as if I had known all along. Mr. Gunther just let out a laugh because no one else got it but us. He took attendance and let me take it to the office. I would help pass out papers—and even help grade them. I got special treatment and it felt good. Feeling confident was new for me. At lunch, he told me I had to eat with the other kids because he had to eat with the teachers. It seemed everybody loved Mr. Gunther. A group of boys sat next to me; the girls stared at me and laughed and giggled. He was right, things sure were different. I hit it off right away with a kid named Danny. He was a little taller than me and had light blond hair and freckles.

After lunch, I started a game of dodge ball and the whole third grade wanted to play. It turned out that I was good and no one could get me out.

After class was dismissed—and it was just the two of us—Mr. Gunther asked, "How was your first day of school, Timmy?"

"Great!" I replied and jumped up and hugged him.

He gave me a note to give to my mother and I asked what it was. He told me to just give it to her. I stayed a little while longer and helped clean up.

When I opened the door to leave, I saw Danny and asked him where he lived.

He said, "On the other side of the school near where you live."

"I just met you. How do you know where I live?"

"I saw you walking across the playground a couple of weeks ago and followed you. Can I walk home with you?"

"Yeah, but let's give this note to my mom and go to your house. Trust me—you wouldn't like my house.'

We talked and laughed until we got to my house.

Mom yelled, "Timmy! Have you seen your room? Oh, you have a friend with you."

"His name is Danny," I said. Then I handed her the note from Mr. Gunther.

She read it and said, "You better not be in trouble."

Danny and I went to clean up my room.

A few minutes later, Mom walked in and asked, "Did your teacher say anything about me?"

I knew where this was going and I played along.

"Yes, he did. He told me my mom was hot."

She smiled and said, "Your room is clean enough."

"Can I go to Danny's house?"

"Not today. You have an appointment with your teacher. He is going to tutor you. When I called him, he told me you knew where he lived."

I smiled and walked out with Danny.

Danny looked at me with wide eyes and asked, "Are you going over to Mr. Gunther's house?"

"Yeah, you heard my mom. He's going to tutor me."

Since Danny's house was on my way, I walked him home. Danny was jealous when I told him about Mr. Gunther's house and the pool and the gym. Wow! What a great day!

At Brian's house, I walked in and he looked at me and smiled. I told him what I said to my mom and he just laughed.

"Then we must keep your mom happy." He looked at me sternly and said, "Timmy, you must never tell anyone about our friendship. People would keep us apart."

I understood what he was saying. "Don't worry. I won't tell anyone."

The next day, three older boys were waiting for me after school. They thought I had wronged one of their little brothers. It wouldn't have taken more than one of them to beat me up, but they all seemed to want in on it. They shoved me back and forth, each getting a chance to hit me. The circle got smaller and more boys could hit me at once. I was being tossed around like a ragdoll. I fought back, but it was useless. A few punches connected with my face and stunned me. I fell to the ground. After several kicks in the stomach, I rolled into a ball. The whole time I stayed strong and didn't cry. They left when they felt their revenge was satisfied.

I got up and went to Mr. Gunther's house. I knew he would be sympathetic—and he was. When he asked what had happened, I broke down and cried. He cleaned me up and told me I would have a black eye. I must have looked pretty bad because I also had a bloody nose, a fat lip, some bruises—and my ribs felt crushed.

I got a lot of sympathy and it felt good for someone to really care. Brian told me he would teach me to fight so it wouldn't happen again. I could work out with him too and he would train me. Boy, did I love that idea! I told him that even if I could fight, they would have still kicked my butt. They were so much older and bigger. He asked their names and I had no trouble giving them up. Then he told me he would take care of everything.

When I went home later that afternoon, Mom was cooking dinner and Dad was watching TV. Mom saw me first and I was shocked at her reaction. "Oh, my God, Timmy. What happened to you?"

Dad and Tommy came into the kitchen to see what Mom was talking about. I couldn't believe it, but they actually really cared. I guess Mom could hit me, but by God, no one else was allowed to. Dad was a big man, and everyone was afraid of him—even me.

"Who did this to you?" he said.

I gave him the names. Tommy knew who they were and where they lived. When they found each of them, Dad scared the hell out of the kids—and the parents. He threatened that if it ever happened again, he would be back to take care of it. That was the first time having him for a dad made me proud.

That night, I was the center of attention—in a positive way—and I didn't even have to eat my vegetables. But that didn't last long.

The next day, some scared, humble kids apologized to me—and word went out not to mess with me. I had a black eye, but I became even more popular that day and that felt good. Even Mr. Gunther got a hold of those kids and they got it from all sides.

After school, I went to Brian's house. I beat him there and used the key he hid for me by the flowerpot. I went in and heard a commotion coming from the kitchen, and I called out, "Brian, I didn't see your car in the drive way."

I walked in the kitchen and I was surprised to see a stylish man around nineteen or twenty with blond hair and deep blue eyes. I froze.

He walked up to me and introduces himself, "Hi, I'm Steve." He put his hands on my cheeks and said, "So you're the new kid. I see why Brian picked you: sandy blond hair, green eyes. Except for that black eye, you would be perfect—just like I used to be."

Right then, Brian walked in and said, "Timmy, my friend and I have to talk." He walked me to the door. "I'll see you tomorrow at school."

I was puzzled at what had been said.

I walked to Danny's house.

He was glad to see me. I met his mom and she looked at me and said, "So you're the legend my son has been talking about."

I smiled shyly. Danny and I went to his room and played cars. It had been a long time since a kid my age wanted to play with me and the time flew by. Before I knew it, it was dark. Danny's mom offered to give me a ride home, but I refused.

She insisted and said, "You are not walking home in the dark. I'll drive you home."

I got home later than I thought and dinner was over.

Mom asked, "How is your tutoring going?"

"Great."

She told me that my dinner was in the oven. I almost walked back outside and checked the address to see if I was in the right house. Mom was being nice and all I could wonder was how long she could keep it up.

The next day, Mr. Gunther lit up when I walked into class, "Timmy—just the man I was looking for."

"Who was that man at your house yesterday? He said he used to be me. What did he mean by that?"

"Oh, Timmy. He's wrong—there could never be anybody like you. He's just a guy I used to know. Believe me—he was never as good as you."

He held my shoulders and looked at me with love and compassion. He'd always had a way with me—and I felt I owed him for my newfound happiness and popularity.

After school, we worked out. I could barely lift the bar that weighed forty-five pounds. Brian could bench 315 for continual reps. I was impressed to say the least. He worked me out hard and we were both sweating. So he took my shirt off and then his. We did a few more sets.

He turned to face me, got on his knees, and undid my pants. He laid me on the workout bench and starting kissing me on the lips.

"Timmy, there could never be another you. Just relax for once and you might like this." He performed oral sex on me, but my body was too young to give him what he wanted.

He stopped and carried me to his bathroom and we showered. We went to the bedroom and he told me he wanted me to do the same thing to him. I didn't know what I was doing, but I did as he asked. He stopped me before he was done and told me how beautiful I was and how lucky he was to have me. When he was finished, he pulled me up to him and we cuddled.

I was always tired afterward and fell asleep. He woke me up and told me it was time for me to go home. I looked up and smiled, what can I say—I loved him. He showed me attention and compassion that I didn't get anywhere else.

At home, the good times were over. The days seemed to repeat themselves as Mom seemed to look for any reason to punish my brother and me. The highlight of my week was going to school and hanging out with Brian.

In October, Brian told me that he had a surprise for me. He was having a barbecue on Saturday and wanted me to come. I didn't want to give in too easily for some reason. I told him I had a lot going on, but he could see right through me. I told him I would be there. I knew my parents would also say yes because they trusted Brian.

CHAPTER THREE

THE DESSERT

I got up early on Saturday morning so I could help Brian get ready for the barbecue and pool party. We mowed the yard and cleaned the pool until eleven. Brian took a shower and I swam until people started arriving. A couple of guys introduced themselves and went swimming with me.

I was getting lots of attention and found out they were a real lively group; laughing, yelling, and having fun. We played volleyball in the pool while Brian cooked. It smelled great and it was going to be the first time that I had ever had steak.

As they divided up the teams, they flipped to see who would pick first. I just knew I would be picked last—as always. I was barely four feet tall and they were all grown men. But I was picked first and it was obvious that the other team wanted me too. I was so surprised and so happy.

When the ball would come to me, someone would pick me up so I could hit it. No one even cared when I missed. When the game was over, one of the guys helped me do flips. I had to show him how Brian did it and he finally got it right. Someone called out that it was time to eat.

As I was getting out of the pool, a guy leaned over and whispered in my ear, "Do you know what's for dessert?"

I shook my head.

"It's you—and I can't wait," he said.

I had no idea what he meant.

I got out of the pool and dried off and became aware of all of the men around me. I got scared as I noticed the way they were talking and looking at me. They were looking at me in the same way Brian did before he wanted sex. I tried to shake it off because I knew Brian would protect me. At least that brought me some peace. Brian fixed my plate and gave me a Coke.

"Brian," I whispered.

"What?"

"Am I okay?"

"What do you mean?"

I told Brian my fear.

"Oh, Timmy. They aren't going to hurt you."

So I relaxed and Brian brought me another Coke. I was never allowed to drink Coke at home so this was a real treat. We got into the pool again and I started acting really stupid. I felt really relaxed and drowsy.

Brian said, "Timmy, you all right?"

I didn't know how to answer and everyone just laughed. Brian picked me up because I don't think I could have swum or even walked by then.

We went to his bedroom and he dried me off and fixed my hair.

"Are you okay?" Brian asked again.

"Yes … I mean no." I shut my eyes.

I felt kisses all over my face and assumed it was Brian, but it wasn't. I could barely open my eyes. When I did, I was shocked that the room was full of men. I don't remember anything after that.

It seemed I slept forever, but then Brian woke me up. My back, butt, and legs hurt. My world was shattered! I asked Brian what had happened.

"Nothing. You started to fall asleep in the pool so I brought you in the house."

I started to cry really hard. Somehow I knew what had happened— even though I couldn't really remember anything. I knew I hurt everywhere and there was a towel with some blood on it next to me.

Brian could see all this registering on my face and he lay down next to me. I turned away from him, but he grabbed me and held me close. He started kissing me.

I said, "Don't, Brian."

I thought he wanted to have sex with me, but he just held me and told me he loved me. We stayed like that for what seemed like hours until the phone rang.

It was my dad calling and Brian asked if I could spend the night.

My dad told him I was to come home. That was the first time I was ever glad to leave Brian's and go home. He helped me get dressed and told me that this was our secret. I thought
Bullshit. I'm telling.
Brian seemed to know what I was thinking. He hugged me close and said, "Timmy, if you tell anyone, they will keep us apart and we won't be buddies anymore. And who will replace you in class as my assistant? I would have to pick another kid. You don't want any other kid taking your job, do you? You know that's what makes you popular."

After hearing that, I had a lot to think about. I told him I wouldn't tell anyone.

Brian handed me an envelope and I asked, "What's this?"

"Open it and find out."

I was shocked, it was full of money.

"What is this for?"

"The guys gave it to you."

It was more money than I had ever seen. I took the money out and laid the envelope on the bed and started counting the bills. Twenty, forty, sixty, eighty, one hundred … then there was a fifty and a hundred dollar bill … five hundred dollars all together.

"We'll go shopping next week. I bet you're tired of walking. Let's go get you a new bike."

I smiled but felt unsure of myself. It was all so confusing, but I guess I could be bought.

We walked to his car and I had to walk slowly because of the pain. "My parents are going to notice."

"Just tell them you slipped off the diving board and hit your butt."

Brian had an answer for everything. As we pulled into the driveway, the lights were off in the house. I walked in and Mom and Dad were watching a movie on the couch.

Dad said, "It's late and you need to go to bed. We're having a family get together at Grandma's and Grandpa's."

I hated going over there but knew I had no choice. They watched me walk by and didn't even notice anything was wrong. I fell right to sleep, but it felt like a truck had run over me when I woke up. I felt like I had been stretched like one of those Stretch Armstrong dolls.

These were my grandparents on my dad's side. They were nice to us and the food was great, but they favored my cousins. Our cousins were older and smarter and enjoyed teasing us. These family events usually ended with Tommy and me getting in trouble with Mom. Somehow my cousins always came out looking innocent. They had no idea that we had gotten the hell beaten out of us when we got home.

As we were walking in the house, Dad finally noticed something was different, "Why are you walking like that, Timmy?"

I told him that I had fallen off the diving board and he believed it without even questioning it. We went inside, but I just went to the den and watched television since I was too sore to play.

On Monday, I felt a lot better but was still walking slowly and carefully. When I got to school, Brian looked at me intently. I knew he was wondering if I had kept our secret. When I reassured him that I had, and he smiled at me.

"This is your day today, Timmy. After school, we will go and get you that new bike."

Since I was still sore, I didn't go out to play at recess. The cool thing was that all the boys were disappointed, reminding me how different things had become. It felt really good to be popular. Usually at recess, Danny and I would be team captains and pick what game we'd all play.

As I helped Mr. Gunther grade papers, I was thinking how good he was with me. He seemed to understand me so much better than my parents did. They wouldn't even spend time with me. The attention I got from my parents wasn't usually positive, but with Brian, I could talk about anything and I never felt stupid. He never rolled his eyes at me. Don't get me wrong, even though I was only nine years old, I knew what he was doing was wrong. I didn't care because it seemed to be a small price to pay. At that time in my life, I really needed his friendship and acceptance.

Throughout the day, he would say things to keep me excited about my new bike. When the bell finally rang, I started to clean up the room like always and he stopped me and told me not today. He told me to walk to his house and he would meet me there. Even though I was sore and he was driving, I still beat him to the house. We were off to the bike shop and it didn't take long for me to find the one I wanted.

Afterward we went out to eat—my treat. We went back to put the bike together. We came up with a plan to explain to my parents that I had won the bike at school because of a third grade project.

This worked because my parents thought Brian walked on water. He would call them often to update them on my progress in tutoring. After the bike was put together, I couldn't wait to ride it. Unfortunately, it still hurt too much to sit on the seat. I opted to go swimming instead and that felt better. I hoped Brian didn't want anything from me. Luckily, he didn't—but he hugged and kissed me and told me how special and good-looking I was.

CHAPTER FOUR

MOM IS BORN AGAIN

I hadn't been home enough to know that Mom and Dad had some new friends. Mom announced that we would be going to church on Sunday. The Pentecostal preacher did a lot of yelling, which didn't bother me because I was used to Mom yelling.

When it was time, Mom was the first one at the altar for prayer. I really didn't know what to think. She stayed up there for a really long time. When she turned around, I could tell that she had been crying. She walked up to me and my brother and dragged us down to the front.

She looked at the pastor and said, "These boys need to be saved."

Yeah, from you!

My brother went with one person and I went with a man named Tony. Tony was tall and skinny with short brown hair. His eyes were hazel and his nose was too big for his face. He was in charge of the kids my age and the group was called Royal Rangers. He asked, "Do you know Jesus?"

"Yes."

"Do you know him personally?"

"No."

We said a prayer and—bingo—I was saved. When the family was back together, it just so happened we all had been saved. I kept thinking that the only one I wanted to be saved from was my mother.

After church, the pastor came over to have lunch with us. He told my parents that we were a wonderful family. He said that the kids behaved so well. I was thinking that it was because we would get the hell beaten out of us after he left if we didn't act right. He even told my dad how proud he must be of his home and family.

On the following Sunday, we went to church—and we began attending on Wednesday nights.

Things didn't get better at home, but they didn't get any worse. The only difference was that Mom was sorry sometimes after beating us. She would say things like she wasn't perfect, just forgiven. Home felt like hell and I hated it. At Brian's, I felt accepted and loved.

My first Wednesday with the Royal Rangers was hard because I didn't know anyone. Tony, the leader, stayed with me to help make it more comfortable. A few times during the meeting, I found him staring at me. I just thought it was because I was new.

The next day at school, we had a substitute teacher. I thought that was strange because Mr. Gunther never missed class. He had left word with the teacher that I would be a big help. The teacher would not tell us why he wasn't there.

Right after school, I ran to his house. No one was there so I unlocked the front door with the key he had left for me. I looked all around the house and found a note in the kitchen. His father had passed away and he would be gone at least a week. I could stay there after school if I wanted, but I needed to make sure everything was locked up when I left.

After the first day, I was bored and I went to Danny's house. When I left Danny's, it was starting to get dark. Tony's car was in the driveway and he was telling my mom about an upcoming camping trip. Even though sign-ups were over, he would let me go if I wanted to.

Dad told me it would be a good idea if I went and made some more friends. I could tell I didn't have a say in this decision. I was going whether I wanted to or not. I agreed and he told me everything I would need to bring.

Tony asked me to walk him out to his car and then he told me what a neat kid I was and what a great family I had. *Boy, have they duped you.* Then he smiled and drove away. I stood there for a moment because it was the look that bothered me again. The look that Brian's friends had like, "You're mine, and you don't even know it."

No way. He's supposed to be a Christian.

Since there would be a lot of other kids on this trip, I thought I would be safe. I still went in the house to see if there was any way out of it, but my parents insisted. I couldn't even talk to Brian about it because he was gone and I wouldn't see him until after the trip.

School wasn't the same for me without Brian; the days seemed to last forever. On Friday, I had to go straight home to pack for the trip. Mom was waiting for me behind the door and I heard a crack and the room went black. She had hit my head with a skillet. I think I only went out for a second or two. The next thing I knew, she was standing over me, slapping me, and yelling, "You don't do shit around here."

She pulled me toward my room and grabbed the broomstick on the way. Each swing found a body part. My back took most of the hits because I had turned away from her. She worked me over good. I wasn't crying and this really pissed her off. I was still seeing stars from the skillet.

My brother walked in and for some reason my mom stopped. He asked if I was all right. He knew the real answer: life wasn't right for either of us.

I just started to cry. I cleaned up and packed my stuff for the trip. Mom walked in and dropped ten dollars on the bed.

She said, "This trip of yours is costing me money I don't have. So you better be grateful. And don't you tell those church people lies about me. I already told them what a liar you are. And you know who they will believe."

I felt like reaching into my pocket and pulling out fifty or sixty dollars and throwing it at her and telling her she could keep her money. She didn't know about the money in my slush fund because I kept most of it at Brian's house. Boy, wouldn't that be hard to explain. So I sucked it up and she left the room.

When Tony honked the horn, I grabbed my overnight bag and sleeping bag and ran out. I threw my stuff in the back of the station wagon and saw he already had a full carload. The kids were already doubled up so I rode in the very back with the luggage. I hoped it wouldn't be a long drive, but I was wrong. It was three and a half hours away. The boys were loud and rude and seemed really put out that I was even there.

It started to rain. From where I was laying I could hear the raindrops. It was soothing and I fell asleep. When I woke up, the sky was dark and the rain had turned to ice. A man was telling Tony that he couldn't drive any farther. The road was flooded out and there was a strong current. Tony was telling him that the bus ahead of him had made it so he was going to try. He put his foot all the way to the floor, the car went down a steep hill, and slammed into a wall of water. The water started coming into the car and all the boys started screaming. The water was almost as high as the windows. The road on the other side had washed away. We hit a rock and the front axle was stuck on top of it. This caused water to come in the back window and all around me.

The tires were peeling out, but we were stuck. I tried to get to the seat in front of me, but the luggage was in my way. The water was up to my chest and the cold shocked me. Tony was yelling for everyone to stay calm and not to panic. Luckily someone stopped the bus in front of us and they pulled us out.

I was the only one that had gotten completely soaked along with the luggage. We were only few miles from the camp and Tony and the others were praising God that he had saved them. I kept thinking that it would have been smarter to have listened to the man and not have driven through the water. I thought I was cold before, now I was turning blue and my hands and feet were numb. When we pulled into camp, snow was falling. When Tony opened up the back door, water poured out. He called my name, but I couldn't even speak.

He lifted me out of the car and handed me to a guy named Ron. I was carried into the meeting hall where all the other kids were warming up and drinking hot chocolate. They took off my shirt, shoes, and socks. With a blanket wrapped around me, I had to take off my pants because they were soaked. They rubbed my hands, chest, and feet to help warm me up. This didn't feel good and all I really wanted to do was go to sleep. I closed my eyes, but some idiot thought if I slept I would die. His mission was to keep me awake. The nurse finally got there, looked me over, and let me go to sleep.

I woke up the next morning feeling great and energized from all my sleep. I only had one problem: I didn't have any clothes on. The only other bed in the room was empty. I could smell food cooking and I was really hungry.

The door opened and Tony asked, "How do you feel?"

"Great! But I'm starved and I need to get dressed."

Tony handed me some of my clothes that had been washed and dried and told me to get dressed. While he waited for me, he apologized for what had happened during the storm. I told him that it was all right. He asked about my bruises, but I just begged to go eat breakfast.

He walked me to the mess hall; when I walked in, everyone got quiet. Then they all clapped for me and I smiled. They even put me at the front of the line. I filled my plate and sat down at the first empty table. The next thing I knew, everyone was starting to sit around me, including some of the kids that had been in the car with me. They started introducing themselves all at once and I didn't know what to do. I just kept on eating.

One kid spoke up and told me about sledding down the mountain and wanted to know if I was well enough to go with him. Before I could answer, I looked up and saw Tony talking to the other counselors and looking my way. I told him I felt great. I wanted to get out of there fast so I wouldn't have to talk to Tony. We raised our hands and were dismissed. While I was putting my tray away, Tony stopped me and told me it was time to talk.

We walked back to the same cabin that Tony and I had stayed in and he asked, "Where did those bruises come from?"

"Are you kidding? I was bounced around in the back of your car with all that luggage. It felt like I was in a blender."

"Bullshit! Those bruises didn't come from the back of my car. They look like someone beat you with a stick."

I stood up, looked him in the eyes, and pleaded, "Just let it go." I knew his dirty little secret. After all I had been through, I could just look at this guy and I knew.

"So you're good at keeping secrets?"

I didn't say anything. My look said, "Of course, can't you tell?" Then I just walked out the door.

Tony stopped me in my tracks. He said, "Timmy, is it your dad?"

"No. It's not! Just drop it. You'll only make it worse."

I hoped that would be all on that subject.

I walked a little farther and the boys were all waiting for me. I felt really good. We walked to the bottom of the hill and they had a van to take us to the top. I thought that was great. We met up with some more kids that were just getting ready to go down the hill. I looked down and was surprised at how steep it was. It had three big slopes with landings so if you were going too fast you could slow down. They had adults at each landing to catch you or just cheer you on as you sped by. Kids were grabbing inner tubes, running to the edge, and jumping off.

Scared as I was, I grabbed one, ran for the edge, and flew off. I held on real tight, but I hit the first landing harder than I thought I would. I almost lost control—even though I wasn't really in control. I continued gaining speed and though it was all over for me. The next two landings were like ramps that put me airborne. When I finally got to the bottom, I was dizzy. I looked back and no one had followed me down. My new friend Mark told me that the hill was for the big kids and we weren't supposed to go down it. I was grateful because I had thought I was going to die.

I headed back to the bottom of the hill and got in the van to go back up again. I didn't know if the boys had tricked me into going down the wrong hill or if they couldn't stop me in time. I just didn't know. But when I got out of the van they were all telling me how cool that was.

The next time, I followed them to the right hill and looked down and it wasn't nearly as bad. We had a blast! Sometimes we would go down the hill with two or three kids at once. Other times, we went down together and just tried to crash into each other. This went on for hours. It was time for lunch and we were so excited they had to keep telling us to be quiet. When we got our food, we all sat at the same table again. I couldn't remember ever having so much fun.

After lunch, we went to one of the cabins that kind of looked like a church. They said it was time for praise and worship and I thought the music was good. There were a lot of kids there from different churches and they were all ages. The preacher was Marcus and he preached fast and hard. I liked it a lot and he really held my attention. Tony made his way to our group and moved the kid next to me so he could sit down. I had been enjoying myself until then.

At the end of the message, he put his arm around me and asked if I knew Jesus. Didn't he remember us having this conversation that one Sunday at church? I told him that I did. Tony asked, "Do you know him personally?"

I looked at him and said, "Personally, I don't know if I knew him personally. How can anyone?"

"It is easy; you have a relationship with him."

"How?"

"You just talk to him and you can tell him anything."

"Doesn't he already know everything?"

"Yes. But he wants to hear it from you. Just tell him what's going on in your life. Tell him you love him and you need him."

If I tell him everything going on in my life, he'll never want to hear from me again.

Since Tony wasn't going away until I prayed with him, I did. I felt the same, but he sure felt better so all was good.

After church, we had arts and crafts. It was getting dark so I knew we wouldn't be sledding anymore. They let us play in the gym until dinner. We played volleyball and to my surprise, I was the first kid picked. It was kind of neat being the new kid after all. After dinner, we had another church meeting and snacks before it was time to go to the cabins for lights out. I really wanted to follow the others and stay with the kids my own age. It made me sad as I walked into the room and I was all alone. I showered, brushed my teeth, and got ready for bed.

Tony strolled in and said, "Timmy, it's our job to go around to every cabin and make sure everyone is in bed and the lights are out. So change back into some clothes and let's go."

I got dressed really fast. It was a lot of fun; I was the only kid with the counselors. Tony let me go into the cabin with our church kids. All the kids had flashlights and were aiming them everywhere. They were all in bed, but I knew they weren't going to go to sleep.

"Hey! What are you doing out of your room?"

"I snuck out to see what you guys were up to," I answered.

"Timmy, you better get back or you'll get in big trouble."

"Don't worry," I said.

Tony came in and yelled, "Lights out and flashlights off."

I walked out with Tony. I couldn't believe how many of the older kids were caught sneaking out. They didn't really get into too much trouble. They were just scared into thinking they might be sent home if they were caught again.

All the counselors got together and went to the kitchen for coffee and cake. I was right in the middle of them and happy. Marcus walked in and poured himself a cup of coffee and everyone took a seat. Tony whispered that I didn't want to be there for the meeting. I went back to the cabin and went to sleep without changing into my pajamas.

In the morning, it was time for breakfast and then church. After that, we got to go sledding again. I thought that I must have misjudged Tony because he was a really nice guy.

The next day, we loaded the car and said good-bye to everyone. We packed ourselves into the station wagon, but I wasn't in the back by myself this time. We sang and laughed all the way home. I was also thinking about Brian and wondering if he would be at school on Tuesday. I wondered if everything would be back to normal—whatever normal was.

I was the last one left to be dropped off and Tony had me sit in the front seat with him. We talked about the highlights of camp like making new friends and sledding down the mountain and being able to check on the other kids at night with him.

Tony asked, "What about giving your heart to Jesus?"

"Oh yeah, that too."

"Timmy, I would really like to help you if you would let me."

"How?" I knew exactly what he was talking about. "There's nothing you can do. We would just stop going to church then you would never see me again. And I would get the hell beat out of me for telling."

"So, you admit to being abused?" he asked.

"Yes! Does that make you happy?"

"No! No, it doesn't." Tony pulled the car over. "No kid deserves to be treated like that. I don't know why anyone would want to hurt you."

I started to cry and said, "Then please, Tony, don't tell anyone."

"Why does your mom let your dad to this to you?"

I laughed—even with tears in my eyes—and said, "It's not my dad—it's my mom."

He had the most unbelievable look on his face, "Your mom? She seems so nice."

I looked him in the eye and said, "Yeah, unless you're her kid. My brother calls her the bitch from hell."

There was a long silence.

"Does your dad know?"

"Yes."

"Well, what does he say?"

"Stuff like, 'just try to stay away from her.' But sometimes you just can't help it. It just happens."

Tony started the car again and I noticed that it was only 1:00 p.m.—way too early for me to go home. Even though it was a holiday,

I knew Dad would be working. I explained this to Tony so he drove me to his house for a while.

I helped him unload all the stuff into his one-bedroom apartment where he lived alone. He went to take a shower and I watched TV, thinking about what a nice guy he was.

His doorbell rang and Tony yelled for me to open the door. It was a man and he just looked at me and walked right past me without saying anything. He walked right into the bathroom where Tony was. I just sat down on the couch and kept watching TV. Then the guy came out and said, "Hi, I'm Paul. Your name is Timmy, right?"

"Yes," I answered and reached out to shake his hand.

"How was your weekend?"

"It was great!"

"Tell me about it," he said. Excitedly I told him in detail about the sledding and not having to walk up the mountain each time and he just laughed.

Tony walked in and said, "Did you tell him you wrecked the front of my car?" The question stunned me. "I'm just kidding, Timmy. Did you tell him how I tried to kill you by drowning?"

"No."

Tony told the whole story—and made me sound brave and heroic.

Paul asked, "Wow. Were you scared?"

"A little."

Tony said, "Are you going to tell your parents?"

"No." I knew the correct answer to that question.

Paul and Tony stared at me for a few moments and I was feeling uncomfortable.

Paul sat down next to me and said, "You're a cute kid."

I didn't even try to comment. Tony turned the television to "The Three Stooges" and sat on the other side of me. The more I laughed, the funnier it made it for them. It was a marathon and we watched it until it was time for dinner.

"Timmy, do you want to eat with us?" Tony asked.

"Sure, if it's all right with you guys."

Tony went to the store for more groceries. "Timmy, how do you like Tony?" "He's great." Then this just flew out of my mouth, "Are you his boyfriend?"

Paul's mouth dropped open and he said, "Why? Would it bother you?"

"No. I was just asking."

He could tell I didn't have a problem with it. "You really shouldn't ask questions like that."

"I'm sorry. Don't be mad."

He answered me by grabbing me and started to wrestle. He acted like I was really strong and almost let me win. This went on until Tony got back. They went to cook dinner and I could hear them talking about what I had said. Tony told Paul about the bruises and stuff. I couldn't hear everything, but I could tell it was about me. I could smell the food cooking and we had chicken, and stir fried rice mixed with vegetables.

I was having a good time with them when Tony let me know it was seven o'clock and I needed to get home. I nodded and got ready to go.

In the car, Tony asked, "Did you like Paul?"

I smiled, thinking Paul had asked the same question. "Yes."

I didn't ask if they were boyfriends this time.

"Timmy, I like you. Let's keep each other's secrets." I smiled and agreed. I thanked him for a great time and made plans to see him on Wednesday at church.

When I walked into the house, everyone was watching television. Dad asked if I had a good time and I told him that I had. I went to my room to unpack and started thinking about Brian. It had been at least a week since I had seen him. The past few days had been so fun and busy that I hadn't even thought about him. This was weird because Brian was the main part of my life—he was everything to me. I felt bad about his dad dying and hoped he was doing all right.

I had a crazy thought about acting like I was asleep and then sneaking out and going to Brian's house to check on him. I stayed dressed under the covers and listened for my parents to go to bed. It felt like forever and I thought I could close my eyes for just a minute. I didn't mean to fall asleep, but I was so tired that I woke up early the next morning. No one was up yet and I was already dressed. Since it was too early for school, I went to Brian's house.

When no one answered the door, I used the key to get in. It was really quiet inside. I looked around for Brian and found him still in bed. He rolled over and was surprised to see me. "Timmy, what the hell are you doing?"

"Are you going to teach today?"

"No. Just go away."

I took off my shoes and crawled into bed with him. He just chuckled and pulled me next to him to cuddle. We both fell asleep for a couple of hours.

I woke up and Brian was reaching for me. I wasn't scared—I had gotten over that. He took off my clothes and kissed my back. His whiskers tickled me and I giggled. He touched me and my body responded for the first time. I wasn't nervous or scared this time.

When he finished, he held me close and told me how wonderful I was. Afterward, he would always tell me how beautiful and wonderful I was.

As we lie there I told him how sorry I was about his dad. Then we were just quiet for a while.

Brian asked, "Did you ditch school today?"

"Kind of—but I am with my teacher."

Brian laughed and went to start the shower. For some reason, showering with him was hard for me. I just wanted to do that by myself. However, I didn't say anything—I just went with him.

We got dressed and, since he had been in the house for days, he was ready to get out. While we went for a drive, I told him about the camping trip and all about driving through the water.

"Is this Tony an idiot? What the hell is wrong with him? He left you in the back seat as it filled up with water?"

I told him how the bus had pulled us out and I had been completely wet and frozen. I had to cut the story short because Brian was so upset. To cheer him up, I told him about how much fun I had sledding down the mountain and this changed the whole mood again.

I looked around and noticed that we were near the beach. I was surprised and he told me he wanted to walk down the pier. We got a good parking place and started walking.

I was quiet and Brian picked up on it and asked, "What's wrong?"

"Nothing"

"Timmy, what is it?"

"Tony knows."

"Tony knows what?"

"Tony knows my secret."

Brian grabbed my shoulders, shook me, and asked, "He knows what about our secret?"

"I didn't say *our* secret. I said *my* secret. You know about my mother—how she hits me." When Brian started calming down, I added, "Brian, I won't ever tell our secret."

As we walked, he told me to tell him everything about the trip and not to leave anything out. I did—in great detail. We sat down on a bench and looked out over the water.

"You really scared me, Timmy. No one can ever find out about us. They'll take you away from me and it will ruin both our lives. You don't want that do you?"

Of course not. I had no problem agreeing to that.

"You know, I hated my dad. He was a son of a bitch and he hated me. We couldn't agree on anything. He never liked any of my friends. I was never going to win his approval or his love. My mom died when I was young. She was the only one who really loved me. When she was alive, my dad and I got along. When she died, that part of him died too. And we've had a bad relationship ever since. I thought I hated him until he died. Hell, I thought he hated me. Then I found out he left everything to me: his house, the cabin in Big Bear, the cars, the boat—even his life insurance money. He left a letter telling me how much he loved me and how proud he was of me."

He sat down on the sand, facing the ocean, and started to cry. I had never seen a man cry before. I put my arms around him doing my best to console him. After about five or ten minutes, he hugged me and said, "Timmy, I can't bear the thought of losing you. I love you."

I hugged him and said, "Don't worry, you won't."

All this time, I had thought he was helping me and I began to realize we were helping each other. We made our way to the car and started back.

Brian stopped at an expensive restaurant and said, "Let's celebrate!"

"Celebrate what?"

"Our friendship."

At dinner, Brian's childhood stories made me laugh. I was having a great time until he said, "We are having a party on Saturday." I stopped laughing and got quiet.

"What? You're not a party pooper—are you?"

"Are all your friends going to be there?"

"Sure they are. And you know what? They have a big surprise for you."

Why didn't he understand that it didn't matter to me?

"What is it?"

"If I tell you, it won't be a surprise now, would it?"

"No, I guess not," I whispered. I was really quiet and in deep thought for a few minutes. "Please, Brian, don't let them hurt me."

"Timmy, they're not going to hurt you. Why do you think that?"

"Because they did last time!"

He looked at me and started eating his dinner again, but he could tell I was still worried.

On the way home, I said, "I like it when it's just us."

"Me too," Brian said. "It will always be you and me, Timmy." I didn't say anything else and just looked out at the landscape. "This will be the last time."

I wanted to believe him, but somehow I knew he was lying. By the time we got to his house, it was dark and time for me to go home. I thanked him for a great day and asked if he was going to school tomorrow. He just shrugged his shoulders.

"If you don't go, I won't either." I didn't know any other way to get to him.

"Bullshit!"

I felt really bold then and asked, "Do I meet you here or at school?"

He looked at me and gave in. He said, "At school."

I laughed because I knew I had him then. I also knew if I missed another day of school, they might call my mother—and neither of us wanted that.

The next day, our whole class was glad that Brian was back. I was wondering if Brian would have quit that year if it wasn't for me. Later on, I would overhear comments and find out I was right. I was the one keeping him there.

Wednesday was a normal day. After school, we went to the house to work out, listen to music, and laugh. My mom called Brian and told him I needed to be home earlier for dinner because of church.

As I went to the front door, Brian told me to have a great time at church.

I stopped and turned to him. "Brian, do you love me?"

"Yes, of course I do."

"Then don't make me come to the party on Saturday. Please!"

"Timmy, do you love me?"

"Yes!" I was pissed off because he had used my line to get to me.

"Then trust me," he said.

I turned around and walked out. I had a lot to think about before Saturday.

At home, Mom was mad because I wasn't early enough to suit her.

"You know it's church night! Why should we have to wait for you?"

I went to my room to change and I got ready. A few minutes later, she came in with a clothesline wire that she had made. I quickly turned around so she wouldn't hit my face and it landed across my back. It hurt so badly, but she was so fast that it landed three times before I could cry out. This was worse than her broomstick or rod. I was crying by the fifth one. For some reason, she stopped and left the room.

I was trying to catch my breath from the pain and crying so hard. My back burned horribly. In the mirror, I could see welts already starting to rise. I heard Mom demanding that everyone get in the car. I put my shirt on and walked out of the house, wiping my tears.

Mom took one look at me and said, "Do you want me to give you something to cry about? No? Then stop crying! Or so help me God, we can go back in the house!"

I quickly got into the car and we drove to church in silence.

As we pulled into the parking lot, we all put on our church faces so nobody would know what life was really like. We got out and went to our own groups. I went to the Royal Rangers, but I was the only one not in uniform—even the adults were wearing theirs. I didn't feel left out though, because the uniforms looked weird to me.

We had a lesson and then it was time for a workshop. Everyone was supposed to get a block of wood and was told to make a car out of it.

Tony had just gotten there because he had been working late. He came up to me and asked, "Where is your wood?"

"I keep it in my pants," I answered and then laughed.

Tony was not amused at all. He said, "We don't talk that way here. How would you like me to tell your mother?"

"I'm sorry. It won't happen again. I hadn't gotten my piece of wood yet," I answered and hoped he wouldn't stay mad.

The project was to build a car and then race it; the best one would win a prize. The winner would race against some other churches and get a bigger prize.

Tony gave me a piece of wood and a kit and said, "This is the stuff you need and it costs $2.50. Do you want me to get it from your mom?"

When I pulled out a twenty, he looked a little stunned. I wanted him not to be mad at me so I wanted to pay for it as soon as I could. He walked back to his desk and left me alone. I looked at the wood, wondering how to make a car. I was clueless.

A friend came over and said, "Hey, Timmy, come to our table and I'll help you."

When we walked back to his table, his dad said, "Sorry, this is a father-and-son project."

I quietly walked back and sat at my table alone until shop time was over. When they said a prayer and dismissed us, I was glad to be leaving.

In the parking lot, we played tag, running up and down the parked cars until our parents came out.

That was a lot of fun. Soon enough, I heard Mom yelling for me. I got in the back seat and Tony appeared out of nowhere.

"Good evening, Mrs. Fielding. I forgot to give Timmy the change I owed him."

Mom didn't know what he was talking about and I was stunned that he would do this to me. He leaned in my window and counted out loud so Mom would hear. Then he said, "We had a problem with Timmy's mouth today." I couldn't believe he was doing this to me.

When he walked away, Mom started the car and drove off. *Oh shit, my life is over!* Tommy's look said, "Nice knowing you."

Mom said, "Timmy, where did you get that money? Did you steal it from me? You stole it, didn't you? Didn't you!

I quickly answered, "You count every penny you have—and you know I couldn't have stolen it from you! I worked for it. I earned it."

She slammed on the brakes and pulled the car over. She reached over the seat and backhanded me a couple of times. I acted like I was crying so she would stop.

I knew I was in really bad trouble. I wondered why Tony had gotten me in trouble. I think he was so scared I would give away his secret. If I had never met Paul, I would have been treated like all the other kids.

When we pulled into the driveway, I saw Dad's truck and hoped my luck had turned around. Dad called out, "How was church?"

"Ask your son!" Mom yelled and then proceeded to tell him the story.

Dad was really disappointed. He said, "Let's start with the money. Where did you get it?"

"I got it working for Mr. Gunther."

"No, he didn't. He stole it from me!"

"I didn't. I got it working for Mr. Gunther."

Mom screamed, "You're lying!"

To my surprise, Dad turned to her and said, "How the hell do you know?" Boy, was she shocked. "We'll call Mr. Gunther tomorrow and ask him."

"You're taking his side?"

"No. I just want the truth."

Mom was steaming and yelled, "Well then, tell him about your dirty mouth."

After she stormed into the house, I explained the story—and told him how I apologized too. He couldn't help but smile a little and chuckle and then he reminded me to watch my mouth at church.

I went straight to my room to get ready for bed. As I undressed, I could hear Mom and Dad fighting.

Dad said, "You better just drop it! Do you hear me?"

Then everything was quiet. As I lie there with the lights off I couldn't believe how Tony had set me up like that.

I was up extra early to avoid Mom that next morning. Brian was still in bed and I woke him up.

He smiled at me and said, "Timmy, you're not supposed to wake me up every morning for school."

I laughed and sat down on his bed and told him about the night before.

"Only you, Timmy," he said and grabbed me in a hug.

I yelled out because it hurt. He lifted my shirt to see how much damage there was.

"What the hell! I thought you said your dad saved you?"

"He did. This is from her being mad before church."

"Timmy, you're a great kid and you certainly don't deserve to be beaten."

He slowly took my shirt off and gently kissed my bruises. I knew what was going to happen next—and I didn't resist. I hardly ever resisted anymore. I just believed he loved me.

Then we both got ready for school. I walked and he drove and nobody was any wiser. When I got to school, Danny was waiting for me like always. The kids treated me great because I was popular and some even wanted to be like me.

If they only knew.

CHAPTER FIVE

SATURDAY, THE BIG SURPRISE!

Brian talked to my parents ahead of time so that I could spend all day Saturday with him—and maybe even the night. I got there as early as I could and he was already working to get ready. I wouldn't let myself think about what might be ahead. I was hoping Brian would watch out for me.

By then, I had cleaned the pool so many times that I was really good at it. I also helped clean the house. When we were done, I put on my suit and jumped in the pool for the first time since the weather had gotten cool. Brian had turned the heater on and it felt warm.

"How does it feel?"

"Great! Come on in."

"Not until our guests arrive," he said.

I was still hoping that no one would show today.

A little while later, some guys walked in—and they weren't alone. They had a kid with them and that really surprised me. Brian called me out of the water.

"Timmy, this is Carlos."

I reached out to shake his hand and asked, "Do you want to go swimming with me?"

Carlos nodded. I jumped back in and he followed.

He was thirteen or fourteen and taller and bigger than me. He had black hair and golden brown skin. He worked out and it showed because he had awesome abs and his chest and arms were defined. He was good looking and confident. We were the exact opposites. My tan had faded and I definitely wasn't confident.

Well, I guess, we are both dessert today.

Instead of putting on swim trunks, Carlos started taking his clothes off. I was totally embarrassed and turned away. He walked to the deep end and dove off the diving board.

He doesn't even care.

I said, "Don't you have a bathing suit?"

"I don't need one. Some of the guys are here already and the party will be starting. What's the matter? Are you embarrassed?" Before I could answer, he tapped me on the head and said, "Tag, you're it."

I took off after him—I didn't even care that he was naked. He was older and stronger, but I gave him a run for his money in the swimming pool.

When the last of the guys showed up, they all took off their clothes and got in the pool. I acted like I wasn't shocked, but I could tell they had all planned it this way. The last time, they had worn bathing suits.

Soon they were all talking in a group and I swam over to see what was going on.

"Let's see who can get Timmy's suit off first."

I turned to the ledge to get out. Someone was close and fast and grabbed my foot. I yelled, but it did no good. I was naked too. I wasn't happy about it and it showed.

"Oh Timmy's mad. Poor Timmy. Don't be mad. This is going to be fun."

Slowly I smiled and said, "Okay, let's play."

We divided into teams and Carlos was one leader and I was the other. Carlos got to pick first and when it was my turn I made sure I got Brian. Then he helped me pick the rest of the team. It was just like last time when the ball would come to me, they would help me put it over the net. They even helped me spike it. Carlos was taller and didn't need any help. Actually, he was quite good. We played four games before the guys started getting tired.

One of the guys grabbed me and said, "Do you want me to flip you like I did the last time?"

I nodded. I knew he was good because I had trained him. He flipped me and I went flying out of the water, realizing that this time I was naked. I was embarrassed, but when I looked around no one else seemed to mind. They liked what they saw. Carlos wanted to be flipped, but he didn't get nearly as high as I had. Another guy got in so they could flip us both at the same time and that was fun. By then, I had relaxed and was having a good time.

A few minutes later, flying through the air, I saw a flash. I realized someone was taking pictures of us. I turned to look at Carlos to see if he knew and I was surprised to see him posing. This sure was different.

Brian and another guy were almost done barbecuing. When Mike and Roger told us that it was time to get out, Carlos swam over to me.

"You're new at this, aren't you?"

I nodded.

"Okay, just play along. If you relax, it won't be so bad—and the pay is great! I've made as much as a thousand dollars. But remember the more you play, the more they pay."

"But aren't you scared?"

"No. They won't hurt you. I promise. Brian won't let anyone hurt you. You're his boy."

"But the last time, they gave me a drink and I don't remember anything after that. I don't know what I'm supposed to do."

"Just do what they say and don't cry. Don't be scared. The money will be worth it. Okay, it's time to get out."

We dried off and kept the towels wrapped around us because it was cold. We went into the house to eat and the food smelled great. I followed Carlos's lead and did just what he said. I laughed at their jokes and played along during dinner. I was sitting next to Brian and Carlos. When I had finished one coke, Brian handed me another cup.

I whispered, "Will this make me sleep?"

Brian laughed and said, "No. But it is wine and Coke. It will relax you."

It tasted pretty good. I finished it before I got up from the table. When I stood, I had to grab the table and catch myself just to get my balance. I did my best to walk straight into the living room. Carlos was laughing behind me.

Mike said, "A little too much wine, I think. I told you that it was more than he could handle."

I just smiled because I felt fine.

Carlos walked up and stood in front of me. Automatically, I backed up a little. He grabbed my shoulders to keep me still and fixed my hair.

Before I realize it, he reached down and took my towel off. I gasped. He took his off and then I look around and realized they were all watching us.

Carlos said, "Timmy, don't look at them. Just look at me."

I nodded. Carlos was a lot easier to look at than the other guys in the room. Brian was built and good looking and Roger was okay looking, but all the others were at best average and some were overweight. It was strange to have all these kinds of thoughts running through my head at once.

Carlos stroked my face and moved his hand to my chest to play with my nipples. I didn't know what to do or what was expected of me. Carlos was ready, and my body had responded and I could see the flash from the cameras. I could hear the comments and knew the guys were happy. They had put a table in the middle of the room and Carlos turned me around to lean on it.

Mike said, "No, Carlos you go first."

As Carlos turned, he whispered, "You know what to do."

We acted out our parts and they gave us instructions.

"Act like it hurts."

"Start fighting to get him off of you."

Carlos and I did our best. I was pretty lightheaded, but I couldn't believe it when I saw a movie camera. I had a flashback to the last party and knew this wasn't the first time I had been filmed.

"Act like you're mad, Timmy. Slap Carlos hard."

I did what he said. This was nothing like what Brian did to me. They stopped us and had Carlos turn around and kiss me. Then they told him to slap me. He did really hard. I just stood there for a second. They told him to do it again and I put up my hand to block this time. They told me not to. I had to just stand there. This time, it hurt so badly that I had tears in my eyes. The next blow hit my nose and lips and they started bleeding. I couldn't believe what was happening.

Someone threw a towel to us so Carlos could clean me up. He gently wiped away the blood and then kissed my lips where the blood had been. He even dried my tears with his hand.

"On your knees, Timmy."

They made us perform oral sex on each other. Carlos liked it, but I was horrified by it. I played my part and Carlos played his until they were done with us. It was the worst experience I'd had with Brian's group. When it was over, all I could do was cry.

I let out a little hiccup from crying and I heard Carlos say, "They'll pay us Timmy."

"How much?"

"You put on quite a show. I imagine a lot."

I gave him a weak smile.

"Let's clean off in the pool," Carlos said.

We played in the water for a while just trying to be kids again, until Roger told Carlos that it was time to go. Carlos swam over and kissed me on my forehead. He said, "It better be a lot because you are worth it."

I looked up and saw Brian watching us.

After everybody left, I sat on the steps of the pool. It was my first time alone all day and I cried with my head on my knees. I was shivering from the cold, but there was a new cold inside my heart that I couldn't explain.

I was thinking about everything that had happened. I wasn't in as much physical pain as the last time, but I still couldn't stop crying. I felt used and dirty. The men had been in control the whole time. It left me completely helpless and that was scary. Until then, I had kept on a brave face.

Brian sat next to me, put his arm around me, and said, "Timmy, what's wrong? You were great. Everybody loved you."

"Then why did you pick Carlos over me?"

"Because, Timmy, I was playing a part. I couldn't pick you and Roger couldn't pick Carlos. Is that what's bothering you?"

I couldn't speak because I was crying so hard. I wanted to explain that I didn't like being used by all those men, but I didn't want Brian mad at me either. I said nothing. He cradled me in his arms and carried me to his bedroom. He dried me off and fixed my hair. He told me how much he loved me and how he wouldn't pick any kid in the world over me. He told me how beautiful and gorgeous I was.

"The first time I saw you at school, you took my breath away. All night, I hoped you would come back—and the next day you did."

Hearing that helped me a lot and I was feeling a little better again. He got up to turn off the lights.

"Aren't you going to lie down too?" I asked.

"No. I have to clean up."

"Let me help."

"No. It would be better if you would just take a nap."

"Please don't leave me right now. Just stay with me until I fall asleep."

He cuddled and made me feel secure again.

I woke up and could smell breakfast cooking. Brian was in the kitchen and he was surprised I was up so early. He told me to go back to bed and brought the food to me. I asked if he had called my parents and gotten their approval for spending the night and he assured me that he had. We sat on the bed and shared the food. It was strange to me because I had never had breakfast in bed before.

"Timmy, about last night, you know how I feel about you. You are a beautiful kid."

"If I am so beautiful, why do people want to hurt me? I feel more like the ugly stepchild that everyone picks on. I'm usually picked last. Kids don't want to play with me and adults want to hit me."

"That's not true. This year you are always team captain and kids like playing with you."

"That's only because of you."

"That was at first. Now you are doing it on your own. You're the most popular kid in the third grade—maybe the whole school. Everyone knows you." I hugged him. I felt like I owed him my life. "As for your family, they are screwed up. All the adults I know love you. What Tony did to you was really wrong."

We sat there for a while I was cuddling under his arm with my head against his chest. "You never asked how much money you made."

"How much?"

"$750."

"You're kidding!"

He told me to get the envelope off the dresser and I counted it out in front of him. Then he told me where the other money was that I hadn't spent and it added up to $870.

"You know you can't tell anyone about this money. It must stay here."

I smiled; boy did I know that was the truth. I asked, "How much did Carlos make?"

"Not as much as you. Everyone put in $100 and that brought it to

$900. There was $450 for each of you, but I put extra in your envelope. So what are you going to do with all this money?"

"I don't know. Can we just go to lunch and go to the movies?"

He smiled. I just loved being able to spend the day with him.

Wednesday came around really fast. I tried to get out of going to church, but no one would hear of it. I didn't want to see Tony or work on the stupid wooden cars.

When I walked in, the kids were standing around talking. One of the leaders called the meeting to order. When I sat down, a couple of the kids moved their chairs closer to me. I looked up and could see that this made Tony and some of the other adults mad. I knew he was turning the other adults against me. After the announcements and a prayer, the lesson began. Tony walked over to me and told me he needed to talk to me outside.

In the parking lot, I asked, "What did I do?"

"I am tired of you giving me dirty looks. Who do you think you are?" He grabbed my collar. I knew his paranoia was getting the best of him.

"No. Please don't hit me. I'm sorry! I'm sorry! Don't hit me." I pulled back so hard I fell to the ground.

People were watching and Tony started to panic. He said, "Timmy, stop it! I'm not going to hit you."

I was crying by then and I whispered, "Please don't hit me."

He leaned over and said, "I'm not."

He stood me up and I saw compassion in his eyes for the first time. He hugged me. I could see over his shoulder and noticed that our whole class had heard and seen everything. Tony took me to a room to talk and asked, "What was that all about?"

"Why do you hate me? What did I do to you?"

"You haven't done anything. And I don't hate you."

"Then why? I haven't told your secret to anyone. You have nothing to worry about. Why did you do that in front of my mom? You knew what she would do to me. You knew I would get the hell beat out of me."

Just then, Mom walked in and said, "What's going on in here?"

Tony jumped up to explain, but it only made things worse. She would never believe I was innocent of anything. One of the parents who had seen the incident in the parking lot had gotten her. She already knew I was in the wrong.

"Don't try to stick up for him! Get in the car!"

It was the longest, scariest walk I could imagine.

In the car, she said, "Don't say a word." Not a problem—I didn't want to make it any worse. I was praying for a miracle and hoping Dad would be home. No such luck. We pulled in and she jumped out and opened my door and grabbed me by my hair. As she was yelling, she was hitting me with her fists and dragging me. I was already crying hard because I knew it was going to be really bad.

In the house, she grabbed the wire and came to my room. She went to work on me. I balled up as tight as I could and got next to the wall to give her the smallest target possible. She realized what I was doing and pulled me away from the wall, but I would roll back as soon as I could. She whipped every limb I had. It took forever, but she finally stopped. I heard the front door close and knew she went back to church to get my brother. I was in horrible pain everywhere—but especially on my back, butt, and legs. I could hardly breathe from the pain. I crawled to the bed and gasped for air. I could feel the wetness of blood mixed with the sweat and it stung. I couldn't sleep and couldn't even stand a blanket on me. I was as hurt and confused as ever. I heard her return and was glad she never even checked on me.

The next morning, I was exhausted from not sleeping. As I tried to take my shirt off, I realized I should have done it the night before. It was stuck to my back with dried blood. I held back my tears and took the shirt off as quickly as I could.

I walked slowly to Brian's house and let myself in. He was just getting out of the shower.

"Timmy, you surprised me."

I lost it and started to cry. It felt good to have someone care about me.

"What's wrong?" He asked as he put his arm around me. I just groaned and pulled back.

"What is it?" He lifted up my shirt. "That bitch! What did she do to you?" He gently took off my shirt and pants to see how bad it was. By the anger he was showing, I knew it was every bit as bad as I thought.

He told me I needed to sit in the bathtub and soak. I told him I was afraid it would hurt, but he assured me that we had to do it to get the wounds clean. He gently lifted me up and set me in the water. After I had soaked for a while, he helped me dry off and applied some medicine to the sores. He brought me a pill and a glass of water. He told me to lie down on the bed on my stomach and he would come back at lunch to check on me. I closed my eyes and fell asleep for the first time. I woke to Brian putting more medicine on my body. He offered me lunch, but I knew I couldn't keep it down. The pill had helped take the pain away so he gave me another one.

I dreamed that Brian was my dad and it was so great that I didn't want to wake up. The smell of food invaded my dream and I woke up and realized Brian was cooking. I made my way to the kitchen.

"Oh, you're up. You act like an old man. You kind of look like an old man."

"It really hurts to put my clothes on."

Brian got one of his shirts for me and it hung down to the floor. I liked it. I sat on a chair and watched him cook. When I came over, he always cooked stuff I liked—just another way to show he really cared about me.

"So what happened?"

I told him everything as I understood it—none of it made any sense to me. But Brian couldn't figure it out either.

"I had a great dream today."

"Yeah, tell me about it."

"You were my dad and I lived here with you. You took care of me and protected me. Can I live here with you?"

I saw tears in his eyes and compassion that touched my heart. "I would give anything if that could happen."

"Then please make it happen."

We both had tears in our eyes.

My walk home that night was slow and measured. When I opened the door, I could see they were already sitting down to dinner. A couple steps into the house and Dad asks, "What's wrong with you?"

"I don't feel too good."

"You better sit down and eat."

Mom said, "Why don't you go lay down. I'll check on you in a little while."

I almost fell over, glad for the reprieve, but knew it wasn't out of concern for me. I took up the offer before they could take it back.

Tom came in a little while later and said, "Mom feels pretty bad about last night. She went back to church to pick me up and Tony told her it was all a misunderstanding. You didn't do anything wrong. This morning, she saw the blood on your clothes and I saw her throw the wire away. Hey, where did you go today? I told Mom you were at school acting like nothing was wrong. But I didn't see you—and when I asked around, they said you weren't there."

"I went to a friend's house."

"You ditched! You better not get caught or there will be even more hell to pay."

Mom walked in and offered a lame apology. She said, "Timmy, I'm sorry about last night. Mommies can make mistakes too. Tony is sorry too—he explained everything to me. You can see how I misunderstood the whole thing. Anyways, he is picking you up on Saturday morning to make up for everything."

Wow, that makes everything better, doesn't it?

The next day at school, Brian helped me take it easy without everyone being able to notice how badly I was hurt. I told him that Tony was picking me up on Saturday and I would let him know how it went.

On Saturday morning, Tony pulled up and I walked to the car. I was still moving a little slowly, but I was more limber than before since the sores were getting smaller. As I sat down in the car, Tony asked, "Do you like to play Frisbee? I thought we might go to the park today."

I knew I was in hell because he didn't even notice anything was wrong. Then he continues to make himself feel better by saying, "I'm glad I got to your mom in time so I could explain what happened. She said she was going home to spank you."

"What? A lot of good that did! You explained after she already beat me. You didn't save me from anything. What did I do to make you so mad at me? I thought we were friends." I took off my shirt and showed him. "It wasn't just my back either. She got my butt and legs too." I wanted him to know what he did to me.

He reached over to put his arm around me.

"Don't. It hurts."

"Timmy, if I could take it back, I would. I don't hate you."

"Then why? Two weeks ago, I said the wrong thing in class. I said

I was sorry. You still told on me. I told you at camp how she was. You knew what she would do to me."

"I didn't mean to, Timmy. It just popped out of my mouth when I saw her. I am so sorry. I really messed up." We sat there quietly for a few minutes. "I know we can't play Frisbee with the shape you're in. I have some friends who have a pool. How does that sound?"

"It's too cold."

"Not this one. It's heated."

We went back to his house and I watched TV while he called his friends.

This one phone call would put into motion a horrible twist of fate.

We pulled up to a very large house and with a landscaped front yard. The guy who let us in was named Todd. He wasn't quite six feet tall, but he was slender and looked scholarly. He had light brown hair and blue eyes. One look and I knew why he was friends with Tony. The house had marble floors and white carpet.

He said, "You must be Timmy."

I nodded and shook his hand.

He asked me to take off my shoes and, while I did, I looked up and froze. Another man was standing there to greet me. He was surprised but quickly covered it. It was Rick—one of the guys from Brian's parties. Rick was over six feet and had a heavier build.

His black hair was longer than Todds' but still well-kept and had brown eyes.

After he introduced himself, he said, "I'll show Timmy where the pool is."

It was the fanciest pool I had ever seen. There was a Jacuzzi in the middle.

Rick said, "Timmy, don't say a word of this to Tony."

I nodded. Tony had left to get Paul and bring him back. Rick took the time to talk to Todd and told him how he knew me. I kept thinking of the irony of pool parties and barbecues with this group.

I heard yelling in the house and I didn't know what to do. I looked at the pool and felt like being anywhere else but here. When the yelling stopped, Rick and Todd came outside, acting like nothing was wrong.

Rick said, "Timmy, your being here has to stay a secret, okay"

I nodded. *Oh great, another secret to keep.*

"Can I tell Brian?"

"No. I can't explain. It just has to be this way. Can you keep it a secret or not?"

"Of course I can. I am the Fort Knox of secret-keeping."

I didn't know what the big deal was.

Todd said, "Let's go swimming."

He didn't have to tell me twice. I took off my shirt right away. "Tony wasn't kidding when he said your mom really got a hold of you."

Rick went into the house and came back with a camera. Todd looked my back over really carefully while Rick took pictures.

Rick said, "Don't worry. I'm a doctor—actually we both are.

Well that explains the fancy house. Drop your drawers. You weren't bashful the other night."

Embarrassed, I did what they said. Rick took more pictures and I pulled my pants back up.

"We have to do something. We have to call the police. We can't just let his mom keep doing this to him," Rick said.

I looked at them dumbfounded. "You can't!" I started running for the gate. Todd caught me and held on. "No. Please don't call the police. You have to let me out of here." I just started crying. Every area of my life was so out of control.

Rick said, "Stop it! Stop it right now! You get over here and we have to talk."

Todd said, "Are you going to run again?"

I shook my head.

"Go and sit down at the table," Rick said. "Now you need to tell me everything that happened."

I took the next fifteen minutes and explained the story. I told them what Tony had done that led to the beating Mom gave me.

Rick said, "Timmy, if you want me to call the cops, I will."

"No. Please don't."

"Then you have to keep my secret, okay?" I knew he was referring to Brian's parties. "Remember that we have pictures of what your mom did to you. We are doctors and the police will believe us. We can go to them anytime. So if you keep our secret, we will keep your secret"

I nodded and wished he knew I didn't need any more threats to keep my mouth shut.

Todd came back with a bathing suit, gave it to me, and said, "Now, let's go swimming."

I smiled. They showed me where I could go change and I was back as fast as I could. I jumped into the pool and found out just how big the swimming trunks were on me. I tied the string as tight as it would go and looked pretty silly.

Todd laughed and said, "Just a little too big, huh, Timmy?"

They laughed and got into the pool. When Tony and Paul came back, Rick whispered, "Act like nothing is wrong."

I nodded and everyone seemed to have a great time after that. I never did tell Brian any of it.

The following Wednesday, I was a little late to church. I was nervous since so much had happened. They started the meeting and I could feel everyone looking at me. When it was time for the workshop, I stared at the piece of wood. The leader made an announcement that we would have the big race in two weeks.

A man walked up to me and said, "I'm Mr. Fletcher and this is Daniel. We're done working on our car and want to know if you want help."

"Yes, sir. My name is Timmy. That would be great."

"We were at camp with you and my son had a great time sledding with you. We'll have a good time doing this. Let's get started."

During the next hour, we got a lot done on my car.

Mr. Fletcher said, "Timmy, we're not quite done. I'll take it home and get the rest of it done for you."

I smiled and said, "Thanks."

I wondered why he was so nice to me.

On Thursday after school, I was taking my usual route to Brian's house when a car pulled up beside me.

Rick said, "I thought I might find you out here." I didn't know how he could have figured that out. He opened the door and said, "Get in."

I did and he pulled away. I wondered why I didn't just run to Brian's house and get away from Rick. I knew I was in trouble.

I truly hated the gut wrenching feeling in the pit of my stomach.

"You had to show up the other day, didn't you?" Rick starts in on me. I was quiet but I was thinking I was never given a choice in the matter. "Todd was so mad he was going to leave me. I just want you to know that you have brought all this on yourself!"

I didn't understand why he was angry and I didn't want to think about what the last threat meant. All I could figure out is that he had to tell Todd about the parties once he saw me.

He pulled up the driveway really fast slamming on the brakes to stop the car and Todd opened my door. I was so scared I couldn't even move.

"Get out," Todd yelled.

When I didn't move, he grabbed my arm and dragged me into the house. No one knew where I was. I couldn't even speak and I was way past crying. Suddenly my head started spinning and I passed out.

I woke up in a bedroom. "Are you going to kill me?" I asked.

Todd said, "Hell no." Then he began to undress me.

I whispered, "Please don't. Why are you doing this?"

With hate and anger in his voice, he said, "You could do Rick and his friends—now it's my turn."

This didn't make sense to my nine-year-old mind. I knew this was going to be worse than anything I had ever experienced. He pulled me to the edge of the bed while I was still on my back. He slapped me a few times and the anger was showing on his face. I was screaming, hoping for the tiniest bit of mercy, but no luck. Every move he made hurt worse than the last until finally it was over. Todd had raped me. I moved away from him and balled up as tight as I could because of the pain. I couldn't stop crying.

Rick walked in and said, "This isn't over yet, Todd. I think the kid still has more in him."

I couldn't believe it. Not again. He wasn't quite as rough as Todd had been, but the pain was still extreme. When it was done, I felt so dirty and sick. Even in the past, my experiences had never left me feeling this used and empty. No one had ever been this rough and cruel with me—Brian wouldn't have let them. This was the first time I had ever felt raped!

Rick told me to get dressed. Their voices were spinning around in my head. I had stopped crying and was trying to sit up and Rick yells again, "Get dressed!" While I was putting on my underwear, Rick shoved some money in my pants pocket. *Like you could put a price on what just happened. No amount of money would make that go away.* I slowly got dressed and carefully walked down the stairs.

They were waiting in the living room for me.

Rick said, "You know this is our secret. We still have pictures of you and we can take it to the police. Hell, we have pictures of you and Carlos. I wonder what your dad would think of that."

I just nodded. I was so defeated. They had made their point a long time ago. All these secrets—all these adults I was protecting—I wondered who would protect me.

I couldn't tell Brian what had happened because they would go to my dad. Someone always had a threat to hang over my head.

And then like a smartass Rick asked, "So is that enough money?" I nodded. "Did you count it yet?"

I shook my head.

"Well count it." I pulled it out of my pocket and counted $300. "Now keep your mouth shut!" I had proven over and over again that I could do that.

Rick told me to get in the car and took me back to the school parking lot. I really wanted to go straight to Brian's house and get some time with him, hoping somehow I could put this behind me. But I knew if he saw me, he would know something was wrong and I couldn't risk that.

The only other place I could really go was home, so off I went at a slow pace. I opened the door slowly, listening carefully for the mood of the house. They were all getting ready for dinner.

Mom yelled, "Timmy, wash your hands for dinner."

I was wondering how I was going to pull this off. Every part of my body hurt and my mind was spinning. I took a deep breath, put on a smile, and headed for the kitchen table. Luckily everyone else had enough to say and Mom was satisfied with me just eating my dinner.

After dinner, I went straight to the bathroom to take a bath. I slipped in slowly letting the warm water hit my skin. It hurt, but I kept going until I was all the way in. The back of my legs hurt; my butt was rubbed raw. I was a mess. *What am I going to do? Who can I tell? Can anyone help me? Can anyone stop them from coming back again for me?* I felt like I was losing my mind. I cried myself to sleep and had the bad luck of reliving it in my nightmares.

I woke up late for school. Mom checked me and said I had a fever and kept me home. When I didn't show up at school, Brian called the house to find out if everything was all right and she explained about the fever. Mom said what a great guy he was. I got to stay in bed the whole day.

Later, the fever spiked even higher and I started throwing up. Mom told me if it got any higher, I would go to the doctor. Just hearing the word 'doctor' put chills up and down my spine. I knew what some doctors were capable of. I kept telling myself that I had to get better. Luckily, it never went any higher. At dinner, Dad announced that the whole family was going to help clean out the garage on Saturday. My heart just dropped—there went my plans to leave early to see Brian.

I left the minute we were done cleaning and got to Brian's as quick as I could. The door was unlocked and as soon as I stepped in, he said, "Timmy, Timmy you're here!"

I felt like everything would be all right. I hugged him tight. I didn't want to ever let go. Brian said, "I have to admit I was nervous when I knew you were stuck in your house for two days. I wasn't sure if you were really sick or if she had hurt you. Was she mean to you?"

"No. She wasn't mean at all. I really did have a fever."

We just hung out at his house that day and it felt good just to be around him.

On Sunday morning, we all got ready for church. I had slipped the $300 in my pocket because I knew I had to get rid of it. I couldn't explain it to my parents or Brian for that matter. I was thinking of putting it in the offering, but people might see me do it. The best plan I came up with was to sneak it into the Bible in the row ahead of us when no one was looking. It was a good feeling knowing someone could put it to good use.

CHAPTER SIX

CHRISTMAS

Christmas was a very special holiday at my house. Mom would decorate every corner of the house and Dad would light up the whole outside. Together, we would make the tree look beautiful. I was looking forward to the two-week vacation because I knew where I would spend my time away from home.

Brian had told me to come early on the first day of vacation. I had trouble waiting for the sunrise. Brian was up and ready when I arrived and he announced that he had a surprise for me. He was going to take me to his dad's cabin at Big Bear that he inherited. We loaded up the car and went up the mountain. The time went by fast. The closer we got, the quieter Brian got. I was sensitive to his moods so I was quiet too. We pulled up to this really cool log cabin.

Brian just sat there, not moving at all. I could see tears in his eyes and one trickled down his cheek. He dried that tear and we started unloading the car. We had brought a lot of stuff and it took us each four or five loads to get it all in. Next it was time to clean the cabin.

"On Christmas, I am going to come up here and spend a few days with my friends." I got quiet because I hated time away from him, especially a couple of days. "Timmy, it's just two days and you will be busy with your family." I nodded—even though I knew I would miss him a lot.

The cabin was in great shape and just needed a light cleaning. Brian was hoping for a fresh snow at Christmas so they could go skiing. Upstairs there was an open loft; it was really large and you could see downstairs. There was a huge bathroom with a Jacuzzi tub.

He started the bath and said, "Let's take a bath."

At this point in our relationship I didn't question the easy stuff. I felt that making him happy was really important. He made it a bubble bath and we had fun with that and laughed a lot.

He said, "If my dad could see me now—if he wasn't dead, he certainly would be. This would kill him. He never liked that I was gay. My dad could be such an ass. He said the cruelest things to me. Mom always had to keep us apart."

I was amazed because that was the first time I had heard Brian say that he was gay.

"Did your dad beat you?"

"No. Sometimes I wished he would have. Then at least … Timmy, your mom's got the patent on beatings."

He smiled to try to make light of the situation. He grabbed my legs and pulled me under. I came up sputtering and smiling.

"Enough about my dad. Let's talk about Christmas. We'll have to celebrate it on another day. I wonder what I am going to get you. Let's go shopping when we get back to town." He pulled me close and whispered, "I am so lucky to have you."

He kissed my neck and then turned me around to face him. It didn't freak me out or anything; I was used to having sex with Brian. He told me it was time to get out of the tub and I thought I had made him mad. He reassured me that he wasn't angry. On the bed, he started to touch and kiss me and then performed oral sex on me. When he was done, Brian laughed. He thought I liked it. And then told me to repeat what he had done on him.

I did my best, but I was still not comfortable or sure of a lot of things. He said, "You drive me crazy." Then he rolled me onto my stomach and began to have sex with me. He ignored my pleas to slow down. When he finally finished and let me go, he realized I was hurting and crying.

"Timmy, I'm sorry. I'm so sorry." He wrapped himself around me to bring back that feeling of safety and security. "Are you mad at me?"

I nodded. Then he started to tickle me and I tried to hold out, but eventually I had to laugh. I wanted to stay mad at him so this wouldn't happen again, but I didn't have the strength. In the end, he always made everything okay for me.

It was time to go back down the mountain to the real world. We went to a sporting goods store and Brian found what he wanted in the skiing section.

I asked, "Can I buy those for you for Christmas?"

"Timmy, they're $350."

"I have more than enough at your house in my slush fund. Who else can I spend it on? I really want to do this!"

Brian smiled and said, "This is too much."

I kept on until he gave in. I felt great buying him new skis.

Our next stop was a toy store. I wanted an electric race car set. I picked out a cheap but nice one. Brian smiled and walked a little farther down the aisle. He bought the best one they had. By the time we got to his house, it was time for me to head home.

"I'm leaving tomorrow morning. But I will set this up for you in the spare room and you can come over and play with it. Just be sure to lock the doors."

"But if you leave tomorrow, that's three days—not two."

"It will go by fast and then we will have the rest of Christmas break to hang out."

I smiled and hung on to that promise all the way home.

When I got home, Dad and Tommy were playing catch in the front yard. Mom was at a ladies meeting. I realized this would be a good night.

Dad yelled, "Guys night out. Let's go eat." Tom and I raced for the car.

The next morning I headed over to Brian's house, hoping I was early enough to catch him before he left. No such luck—the house was empty. I went to the spare room and he had taken the time to put the whole track together. I played with it for a few hours, acting like I was a famous race car driver. When I started getting lonely, I headed for Danny's house.

He was glad to see me and the time with him would make the days go by faster. I told him about my race car track. He looked amazed. When I told him it was at Mr. Gunther's house, he didn't believe me.

"Let's go and I'll show you. It's really cool."

"Don't you need to ask permission before I come over?"

"No. He isn't even home right now. He's out of town until after Christmas."

Danny was confused, but thought it would be really cool to get to go to Mr. Gunther's house. It would give him something to talk about when school started again.

We had fun walking to the house. I enjoyed hanging around someone my own age again. I was shocked to see a car in Brian's driveway. Danny and I hid behind some bushes until I could figure out who it was. The car looked familiar and I wasn't sure what to do.

When I decided to go inside, Danny followed.

That is when I realized how bad my luck was. The person walking out was Rick. He looked at me and said, "What are you doing here?"

Feeling kind of sure of myself, I said, "I'm always here."

I looked at what he was carrying out of the house.

Rick said, "I'm picking up this box for Brian."

He took a long look at me and Danny and walked to his car and drove off. *What an asshole.* Even though nothing happened, I found myself a little shaky just from being around him. I really thought he had been there looking for me, but I had no way to prove it.

I took Danny to the room where my race car track was and we played for quite a while. Danny looked at the clock and said it was time for him to go home. It was still too early for me to chance being home so I played with my toys a little longer.

I heard the door open and jumped. I turned around and knew I was in trouble. Rick had come back. I stood there kicking myself for not leaving when Danny had. Even going home was a lot better than what could happen with Rick.

I tried to play it off by saying, "Did you forget something?"

"Yeah I did—you! Get in the car."

I was terrified. I knew I didn't have a chance of outrunning him. I slowly walked to the car. Rick locked the house up. I felt like throwing up but knew that would only make it worse. I could tell Rick was really mad. I took a chance to ask because maybe I could fix it.

"Rick, what's wrong? Why are you mad?"

"Did you tell your friend?"

"No!"

"Then why was he acting so weird?"

"I don't know. I swear I haven't told anybody anything. I haven't even told Brian. Aren't you going to the mountains with the other guys?"

"Yeah, but that's tomorrow."

"How did you find me?"

"I always know where you're at."

I didn't know if that meant that Brian had told him where to find me, but I knew Brian loved me. I didn't think he would do this to me.

Todd was waiting in their driveway. He grabbed me and started to drag me out of the car.

"No need to do that. I'm already here. Like I could really get away from you guys."

I walked ahead of them and opened the door to go inside. I knew what they wanted, but I was hoping for a miracle.

I was waiting for some direction in the living room. Rick leered at me and told me to take off my clothes. All I could think was how I could stand in front of them naked.

I guess I wasn't moving fast enough because Todd hauled off and slapped me hard. I fell to the ground, holding my face. Rick threw me over his shoulder and carried me upstairs. I felt small, weak, and helpless—and they hadn't even begun yet. I couldn't believe what I saw. It was a scene out of a bad horror flick. There were restraints hanging from the ceiling and I froze with fear. I just stood there and Rick undressed me.

He tied my hands to the restraints and made it high enough that I had to stand on my tips of my toes. It hurt and I was cold, naked, and scared out of my mind.

Todd walked behind me with a paddle and hit me lightly. It was more scary than painful.

"Who did you tell?" Rick said.

I pulled to see if I could free my arms. No such luck. I told myself that I couldn't panic. I had to hold it together. I said, "I haven't told anyone."

Without warning, Todd hit my butt really hard. I jumped because of the pain. I knew I was at their mercy and that was the most horrible feeling. I had tears in my eyes as the panic was rising—and he hit me again. Now I'm begging. "Please stop. You know I haven't told anyone. I don't tell secrets. I know better."

Rick pulled out a blindfold and put it on me. I was really scared now. Not being able to see what is coming put my mind over the edge. They hit me a few more times—not too hard—it was almost like they were teasing me. A really hard one landed and I yelled loud! Not knowing what was coming next, my instinct was to flinch each time they touched me. I was dangling from the ceiling, on my toes, scared out of my mind, and in pain. *Could anything possibly get worse than this?*

Finally they left me alone and I could hear them next to me on the bed. I knew what those sounds meant. I hoped it meant they wouldn't need me anymore. I lost all sense of time. It took all my strength to stay up on my toes so I could breathe.

Finally, Rick and Todd were finished. Rick got up and took off the blindfold while Todd undid the restraints. I fell to the floor; my arms and hands were completely numb. My legs were weak from supporting me.

Rick said, "We are going swimming. Come down when you're ready." Just like that—like nothing was wrong, or weird, or freaky. *What the hell is wrong with these guys?*

I finally went downstairs.

Rick asked, "Are you ready to go in the pool?" I shook my head. All I wanted was to get out of their house as quickly as possible. I would have walked home if I knew the way. "I think you do. Let's go."

I guess we were going swimming. I hoped this game wouldn't be as freaky as the last one.

Rick and I started swimming and Todd asked if anyone was hungry. We both replied yes. Rick swam over to me and I got really nervous.

"Timmy, relax. We're done. Nothing else will happen to you ... that you don't want. We would never hurt you. It's just a game and you'll get paid for it. Look, we didn't even leave a mark on you. It didn't hurt, did it?"

I was thinking that I heard this way too much from adults. I shook my head because he didn't want to hear the truth.

Rick swam to the Jacuzzi and motioned for me to join him. He sat down quickly, but I had to work my way slowly because it was so hot. Rick looked at me while my body was still mostly out of the water. He said, "Timmy, for a kid, you're perfect."

"I think Carlos has the perfect body." I couldn't believe that actually had come out of my mouth.

Rick laughed and said, "That's because he is older and works out."

"So do I. I work out with Brian. Everyone knows he works out and he is in better shape than any of the other guys."

"You are just younger than Carlos and your abs look great. Flex for me." I stood up and flexed. "See you have a good set of abs. How did you meet Brian?"

"He's my teacher."

"Yeah, I know that, but how did you meet him? How did you get to be buddies?"

I told Rick how we had met at school last summer and all the major points until we got the okay from my parents for tutoring. It was easy talking with Rick. I wished he had treated me like this before. I felt like a real person—not just a piece of meat.

I had gathered enough confidence to ask Rick, "Why are you so mean to me? What did I ever do to you?"

Rick stops and thinks. He was surprised that I actually asked him and I think he felt I needed an answer. "I guess it's because I'm jealous."

I was floored, "You're jealous? Jealous of what?"

"You are young and good looking and everyone in the group wants you. When you walk in the room, you're the center of attention. And you aren't mine, you are Brian's. But, I have you just the same, don't I?"

I nodded. He had me anytime he wanted to drive by and pick me off the street—like a thief in the night.

Since we were talking like friends Rick felt the need to apologize and says, "Hey, Timmy. I'm sorry."

"You guys really scare me. I'm still nervous from what happened upstairs."

"It's just a game. I would never hurt you. Not too much anyways."

That didn't make me feel a whole lot better.

Todd yelled that the food was done and we got out of the pool. I put a towel around my waist and followed the guys inside. Rick and Todd started talking about work and stuff going on at the hospital. I was glad that their attention wasn't on me any longer. Rick looked over and told me to get dressed. This was good news and bad news. The good news was I could put my clothes on and go home.

The bad news was that they were up in the bedroom where the

black leather restraints are hanging from the ceiling. I opened the door nervously, grabbed my clothes, and took them to a bathroom down the hall to change. No one had even had sex with me this time, but it messed with my mind just the same. I walked to the bottom of the stairs and Rick put some money in my pocket.

"Timmy, this is our secret." I nodded, but that wasn't good enough. "Say it. Just say it."

I replied with as much conviction as I thought they needed, "It's our secret."

Rick took me back to school and I walked home. When I walked in the door, Tommy pulled me into his bedroom. He asked, "What did you get Mom and Dad for Christmas?"

"Nothing yet."

"Let's go in together on something because I only have ten dollars. How much do you have?" *Now that's a tricky question. Do you mean what is at Brian's house in my slush fund? What is hidden in my pocket that I haven't even counted yet?*

"Let's go to my room and I'll check."

"Hurry. Mom wants to go shopping now."

I pulled the money out of my pocket, hiding as much as I could. "Holy shit. How much do you have?" It was $300, but I only told him $100. "Where did you get $100? Did you steal it?"

"No, I didn't steal it. I got it working for Brian. But this is our secret, okay? I'll give you half, but you have to keep it a secret."

"Are you sure you didn't steal it."

"No. I earned it." He would never know what that really meant.

During this time of year, my mom stayed happy so we took full advantage of that. The whole family went shopping and Tom and I got our parents some really great gifts.

The next Sunday, I put the other $200 in a Bible. They all looked the same, so I never knew if it went to the same person. It was strange because what was a blessing to them was pure torment from hell for me.

Once Christmas was over, Brian was home. I headed over there early every day and stayed as late as I dared. Brian had bought me more gifts that I could keep at his house. I was enjoying the relaxed feeling of spending the days with Brian.

He asked, "What's your family planning for New Year's Eve?"

"Mom and Dad are going out with friends. Tommy and I are staying home."

"You've got something important to do that night for me."

I was hoping it wasn't another party. "What?"

"There is a big New Year's Party. You need to go with me."

"Well, I don't know if Mom and Dad will let me stay out that night?"

"You better convince them! With a New Year starting, I can always look for a new kid." This threat got me every time. Brian could replace me, but I could never replace him in my life.

"Is it going to be here?"

"No—at a friend's house." It would be at Roger's house. "Don't worry. Carlos will be there." I must have given him a funny look. "You like Carlos, don't you?"

"He's all right."

"What do you mean? I thought you guys hit it off last time."

"We did."

"Don't you want to see him again?"

"I don't know."

"What do you mean by that? Don't you want to go?"

I wanted to be around Brian and Carlos, but the other part scared me. I didn't know how to explain that. I just looked up into his eyes and hoped he saw the truth.

I said, "I just want to be with you."

Brian smiled and said, "I like that answer. I really do love you." He hugged me tightly and kissed the top of my head—then walked back to his bedroom.

CHAPTER SEVEN

NEW YEAR'S EVE PARTY

On New Year's Eve, we got to Roger's house at seven o'clock. It seemed like most of the people were there already. He had an awesome house on a hill with a great view of the city. Carlos met me at the door and was excited that I had finally gotten there.

"Let me give you the grand tour."

It was huge. It even had a movie room. Carlos showed me his bedroom and I asked, "You live here?"

"Yeah."

He had a TV and an expensive stereo—all the new technology a teenager could want.

I knew he looked nothing like Roger so I asked, "Is Roger your dad?"

Carlos laughed. "No. Not like that. He knows my family in Puerto Rico and they wanted me to live in the States. He's kind of like an uncle."

I nodded that I understood.

At the pool, another kid walked up to us. Nick was twelve and about as big as Carlos but was slender and had curly blond hair. His eyes were a deep blue and his face was masculine. I hoped maybe he was a new kid. I could tell by the way they were talking that they were old friends. I was the new one once again.

Nick asked, "Are we going swimming now?"

Carlos said, "Yes."

They both took off their clothes and dove in.

Carlos swam to the edge and I asked him where the bathroom was. He pointed to a door. I went into the bathroom and closed the door.

I looked in the mirror and thought, *How am I going to get through this?*

I slowly took off my clothes and I stood there arguing with myself. I must have been in there a long time because Carlos said, "Timmy, are you in there?"

"Yes."

"Let me in and we'll talk." I unlocked the door. "What's wrong?"

"There are a lot of people here and I'm scared. You and Nick know what you're doing. I don't."

Nick knocked on the door and came in.

Carlos said, "Timmy is scared."

Nick said, "I thought you said he did great last time and that he's really good. Carlos just looks at him as if to say look at how young he is, what do you expect? Nick looks at me and says, "Don't worry. We'll help you. It's all a game."

Carlos put his arm around me and said, "Yeah, don't be scared—just stay with us." He grabbed my arm and pulled me out the door. "Come on. Let's go swimming. We have men to entertain."

Nick laughed and they both grabbed an arm. We ran naked to the pool and jumped in. We were a pervert's dream.

The water was warm, but the air was cold. I swam because I thought that was what was expected of me. It wasn't long before the men started to join us. That's what all the parties were about—men with boys.

Nick and Carlos did what they said and one of them always stayed by my side. We swam and played games for a while and a few men got out of the water to cook. The pool party ended with the men flipping us through the air. I could still go the highest because I was the lightest. Sometimes I could even do a double.

When it was time to get out, I was scared. All the parties were the same for the first part. We would swim, play, and eat—but I knew from experience that anything could happen after swimming. That part was never the same. *Here we go. I hope Carlos and Nick can still keep me safe.*

Brian was busy with the cooking and Carlos made my plate for me. This made me feel good for some reason. Carlos and Nick were having fun talking and Carlos saw me thinking too hard. He leaned over and said, "Timmy, it's just like last time. We're going to act and we're going to get paid really good for it. Just do as you're told and don't ask any questions. And don't cry."

Nick said, "Let him cry—we'll get more money."

Carlos gave him a dirty look that said shut up. Nick was the obnoxious one of the group. "Timmy, don't panic. Just remember it's a game."

"What are we going to do?" I hoped Carlos would know something.

"I don't know. They never tell us. But it's already planned out and you just need to do what they say."

There were a lot more men at the party because it was New Year's. What a strange way to start a new year. Brian walked up behind me and whispered, "How are you doing?"

Carlos said, "Don't worry. We're taking care of him."

Brian smiled and said, "I knew you would."

They moved the tables and chairs out of the dining room. The living room furniture had been moved before the party even started. Plastic sheets covered the carpets. I had seen it earlier and thought it was because people can be messy eaters. I was to learn that they needed it for what was going to happen next. We were told to take our towels off and to rub baby oil on each other. Nick and Carlos made this fun, but I could hear that it was driving some of the men crazy already.

The next thing we had to do was to take turns wrestling. Carlos beat me easily because it wasn't an even match. Carlos beat Nick easily—even though he was bigger. Nick had no trouble beating me. So they teamed me and Nick against Carlos and this was the closest to a fair fight. Finally Nick and I pinned Carlos down and everyone clapped.

Roger called out for Nick to kiss me. Nick gently leaned over and kissed me on the lips. Roger specified that it was time for a French kiss. I didn't know what that meant. Nick put his mouth over my top lip and my bottom lip and put his tongue in my mouth. I jerked backward, but he grabbed the back of my head.

He whispered, "Just go with it."

I followed his orders. Next, they wanted Nick and Carlos to make out and they put on a good show. I could tell they weren't even nervous. It was hard for me to watch because I thought it was gross. I could see that Nick and Carlos were getting excited. I looked around the room and I was the only one not physically excited. Roger called out for me to get involved.

A table was brought in to the middle of the room. Roger told us what to do and we had sex with one another. This got the men really excited. Roger told me to slap Carlos really hard. I looked over at Carlos for help, but he nodded for me to continue.

Nick said, "Well?"

I did what I was supposed to and this drove the men even crazier. Roger told me to slap Nick. I hesitated and this made everyone mad.

"You're supposed to do this without question," Carlos said. "Hit him."

I hit him lightly and this enraged the men.

Someone said, "You hit like a girl."

Roger said, "Nick, show Timmy how to do it."

Before I realized what was happening, Nick slapped me hard.

"More," Roger said.

Nick hit me again and again. My lips start to bleed and Brian said, "That's enough."

Tears were rolling down my face and Roger said, "Now slap Nick."

I hit him hard enough that no one complained. Then the men got their turns until they all got what they wanted.

Carlos took me to the bathroom and cleaned my face. I appreciated him taking care of me like that. I didn't feel so alone. We decided we would go back in the swimming pool to play. We could have our own fun now that the men were finished with us.

Midnight came and went and then the party broke up. I was talking to Carlos when Brian came out of the movie room. I was so tired that I had a hard time staying awake. Brian told me we were spending the night. He told Carlos to take care of me. Carlos was glad I was staying.

All I wanted to do was close my eyes. Carlos took me up to his bedroom and we crawled into bed. When I woke up, I saw Carlos and remembered where I was.

Carlos whispered, "Are you awake yet?"

"Yes."

"Guess what? Roger and Brian are going to take us to Venice Beach."

I liked that idea a lot because I liked being around Carlos. He picked out some of his clothes that could fit me and threw them at me.

He said, "Let's go take a shower."

We went to the bathroom and Carlos set the water temperature. I still felt weird in these situations. It was strange being naked and showering with someone, but I didn't say anything. I thought what the hell; we'd seen each other before and done everything to each other. Being bashful now seemed stupid.

I stepped under the water and started shampooing my hair. Carlos took over and did it for me. It felt weird but kind of good too. He told me to wash his hair and I did. He washed my whole backside and turned around for me to do the same. I didn't feel good about this, but Carlos acted like it was normal. What was normal anymore? After the shower, we both got out and dried off. I started to get dressed, but Carlos stopped me.

He said, "I have to get some release or I'll be horny all day. Do you know what I mean?"

I really had no idea what he meant, but I went with it. When he was done, Carlos was really happy. I was too young for it to make sense. We got dressed and I really liked the cool clothes that he had picked out for me.

Carlos went downstairs ahead of me and was talking with Brian and Roger. When they saw me, they started laughing.

Brian put his arm around me and said, "That's my boy."

I was totally confused and this made them laugh even more.

Roger had a convertible and we all piled into it and had a great ride to the beach. When we got out of the car, Carlos reached over and held my hand. I was still young enough that it didn't create any attention. Brian and Roger were walking ahead of us, looking at the sights.

Carlos said, "You're lucky you have Brian."

"Are you lucky to live with Roger?"

"I'm not sure anymore."

"Yeah, I am. Did you know that Roger and Brian are going out?"

"No. I didn't." I was kind of shocked.

"Since Christmas! They got together when we were in the mountains."

"Did you get to go?"

"Yeah, you know. Now we are kind of like brothers."

That made me smile.

We stopped at an outside restaurant and watched the people while we ate our lunch. At Venice Beach, there were vendors and shops and entertainers all along the sidewalk. There was always something to see or do. Brian and Roger had fun trying to get the vendors to drop their prices—even though they could afford to pay full price. I was content just to walk with the group. Carlos found some cool shirts to buy. Then he bought both of us some really cool necklaces.

Brian asked if I wanted to buy anything. I told him that I didn't have any money. Brian laughed and said, "Timmy, you're loaded."

"I am?"

"You made $600 last night. How much do you want?" I shrugged my shoulders. Brian handed me $100 and said, "If you need more, let me know."

I bought a couple shirts. I really liked Carlos's style. He found some sunglasses, but I bought them before he could. We shopped so long that I was getting really tired. Brian picked me up and put me on his shoulders. I could see everything from up there. It was great.

We headed back to Roger's house and I fell asleep on the way. Brian must have carried me to his car and into the house. He woke me up at his house and told me it was time to go home.

"Brian, I had a really great time today."

"That's what I love about you—no matter what happens, you are always grateful."

I smiled and start walking home.

I opened the door slowly, hoping that the Christmas holiday cheer would last through the New Year.

Mom yelled, "Where the hell have you been? I work around here all day and night cooking and cleaning! You don't call or nothing! You just show up when you want to! Dinner was ready hours ago! You little shit!"

She pulled out a belt from behind her back and slapped me across the face with it. I put my hands up to block—and that really pissed her off. After a couple more swings at my face, she reverted to her favorite weapon: the broomstick. I took a few steps away before she got in her first hit. My back took the full pounding. I fell to the floor to make a smaller target. She worked me over from top to bottom. I balled up tight and cried.

Her arms finally got tired but her rage was still going. Mom yells at me, "Now clean the kitchen, you ungrateful little brat!"

I stood up, still crying because the pain went from my head to my toes. There was no end to this night. The kitchen looked like a war zone. My mom could make the biggest mess when she cooked. It took almost an hour and a half just to wash the dishes.

She came in and looked at a pan that I had just gotten done with. "You call this clean?" Then she hit me on the head with it! I couldn't believe it. My ears were ringing, my neck snapped back, and I dropped to the floor. "I'm sorry, Mom. I'm sorry. I'll clean it again."

This made her madder and she hit me all over with the pan. It was heavier than the broom and her arm tired faster. I finished cleaning the kitchen with a really bad headache. My neck was killing me and my body felt like it had been run over by a truck. I was hoping and praying that I could get everything clean enough for her.

I headed for my bedroom as soon as I could—only to find that she had dumped out every drawer I had. And she had thrown everything out of my closet in the middle of the room.

"Your room is a mess! You clean it right now!" She stomped out of my room and went into her room. I spent the next couple of hours putting everything back where it had been—making sure I could make everything as perfect as possible.

Tommy walked in and said, "Mom is such a bitch. I can't wait until I grow up and move out of here."

I could tell from his bruises that she had gotten a hold of him also. His face and arms looked pretty bad. There was no telling how many bruises were under his clothes.

On my way to Brian's house on Saturday morning, a couple of high school boys grabbed my arms and dragged me to an empty field. They shoved me from one to another saying, "So you think you're tough, huh?"

I was thinking, *Heck no, I'm not tough; I'm only nine years old.* By now I know I have a sign posted on my forehead for all to see that says Hit Me. I tried to tell them that they had the wrong guy. They made a circle, bouncing me off each other until I fell to the ground. Once I hit the dirt, they started kicking me like a soccer ball. I covered my head and balled up, but the blows were coming from all directions.

I was begging them to stop, but they didn't even hear me. A gruff old man walked out of his back door and threatened to call the cops on us if we didn't get the hell away from there. The boys gave me one last kick and took off running.

The old man told me that I had better leave before they came back. I totally agreed. I stood up and dusted off my clothes. I was filthy and had trouble standing straight. My stomach was the worst because they had kicked me over and over again. It was hard to catch my breath.

Brian's door was locked so I looked for the key. It wasn't there so I knocked on the door. There was no answer so I tried the back door. That was locked also.

I knew I was not going back home. I took my shirt off to get it wet in the pool. I decided it was easier to get into the pool to wash off.

The air was cold, but the water is warm. I took off my clothes and get in to clean up. I could feel myself getting ready to throw up and I made my way out of the pool and behind the pump. It hurt really bad to throw up and I saw a lot of blood mixed in it. That really scared me and then the world went black.

I woke up at Rick and Todd's house with Brian next to me on the couch. It took me a minute to figure out what had happened.

Brian asked, "Are you all right?"

I tried to sit up, but pain shot through my stomach and ribs. I looked over and saw Roger and Carlos. I was really confused about how everybody had gotten there.

"Timmy, are you all right?"

I just nodded.

Rick said, "He's lucky this time. His ribs aren't broken, but they may be cracked. We need to take him to my office for X-rays."

Brian said, "This can't keep happening! Your mom has to be turned in. She could kill you."

I mumbled because I couldn't get enough breath to talk loud. "It wasn't her."

"What?" Brian asked.

"It wasn't her. I got jumped by some high school kids on my way to your house."

"Don't keep lying to protect her."

"I'm not."

I didn't have the energy to explain the beating in the kitchen. I know the injuries were from both beatings. Brian sounded serious about turning my mom in this time. If that came out, I might lose Brian too. Brian and the guys went into the kitchen to decide what to do.

Carlos said, "Timmy, you're lucky I found you. I thought I heard you knock, but by the time I got to the door, no one was there. I didn't see you in the back, but I saw the water on the cement from the pool. I knew you had to be out there somewhere. Then I saw you lying there. It scared me because I was afraid with all that water you would get shocked by the electric pump. I yelled for Brian and Roger." I knew why I couldn't find a key or any other way to get in the house. Brian didn't want me walking in on him and Roger. "You were cold as ice. Your head was near the vomit and we saw the blood. We rushed right over here. What really happened? Did you get jumped?"

"Yeah, I really did get jumped. I'm not lying. Please believe me."

Carlos leaned over and kissed my forehead. "I believe you, Timmy. You need to rest now."

Carlos went to the kitchen to tell them about our talk.

Brian said, "We won't call the police this time, but you have to tell me what really happened."

It was frustrating for me but I had been beaten so many times by Mom that they were having trouble believing me.

"I got jumped, Brian. You've got to believe me." I begged for him to understand.

Rick said, "It really doesn't matter now. We are going to treat the injuries as best we can. Here is a shot for the pain and we are going to get X-rays."

Within a few minutes, I was out. Everything after that was a blur. When the medicine wore off, I woke up on Brian's couch feeling a lot better.

Brian said, "Back from the dead. What you will do for attention."

He had no idea what I would do for his affection and his attention. I would willingly take a hundred beatings if it would bring me closer to him.

Brian said, "It's getting late. Call your parents to see if you can spend the night at Danny's."

Once again, we were using poor Danny.

I got mentally ready for the call and made my voice perky.

Tommy answered and said, "You better get home."

"Ask Mom if I can spend the night."

The next thing I knew, Mom was on the phone wanting to speak to Danny's mom.

"Danny's dad is here. Can you talk to him?"

I handed the phone to Roger because she knew Brian's voice. He played it off and got her to agree to let me spend the night.

When he got off the phone, he said, "You put me on the spot. I don't like that."

Brian said, "But you did so well."

We all laughed. I stopped quickly and learned my ribs couldn't handle that yet.

Brian said, "How do you feel?"

"Kind of like a truck hit me."

"I bet. But you lied to me. When you were on morphine, you told the whole story." Tears welled up in my eyes. "Now tell me the truth."

"But you already know it."

"I want to hear it from you when you're not on morphine." I explained the whole story starting with Mom beating me in the kitchen and ended with the teenagers kicking me in the field. "Who are these guys?"

"I don't know."

"Timmy, you have to tell me who they are."

"But I really don't know their names."

"Okay, but we have to find out who these kids are. They can't get away with this. Are you getting hungry yet?"

"Yeah, I'm starved." I tried to sit up, but he stopped me. I am glad he did; my head felt fuzzy and my sides hurt every time I breathed.

"I'll bring it to you."

I wanted to ask him why I couldn't find the key, but I chickened out. I don't know if I could have handled the answer. Carlos brought a checker board and we played. I was winning all the games and figured Carlos was doing that to make me feel better.

When dinner was done, they brought their plates into the living room and they ate with me. After dinner, Roger and Carlos had to go home. Brian carried me to his bedroom and put me gently on the bed. I felt like all was right in the world for a little while. I watched TV until I fell asleep.

The next morning, I realized I had slept in. This wasn't something I could do at my house.

Brian was still asleep. I had to go to the bathroom. I rolled as gently to the edge as I could and stood up slowly. It hurt a lot, but I knew I had to move. It hurt to pee and I must have been in there for a long time.

Brian asked, "Are you okay?"

"Yeah."

When I finally got out, he said, "Are you sure everything's okay?"

He looked so concerned. I gave him a nod and a weak smile. I didn't want to tell him about the blood.

"Rick and Todd want to see you this morning."

"Why do they want to see me?"

"Maybe the doctors are worried about you."

At least he referred to them as doctors. I knew they might not want anything from me.

"What's wrong with me?"

"Nothing is wrong. We are just being cautious."

"I—"

"What?"

"I just don't feel good."

"That's why we are going there—so they can check you out again and make sure nothing is wrong."

"I don't want anyone touching me."

Brian is confused and answers, "They are doctors, Timmy. They have to touch you. I'll be there with you and no one will hurt you."

I felt better, but Brian had no idea what Todd and Rick had been doing to me.

On the way over there, I wanted to make sure Brian understood how I felt.

"Brian please don't leave me alone with them"

"Carlos will be there."

"I don't feel good. Please don't leave me. I want you—not Carlos—not anyone else. Just you."

I could see that made him feel important. "Don't worry, Timmy. I won't leave you and no one will hurt you."

Finally satisfied, I let it go and soon we arrived at their house.

It was hard getting out of the car. I had to do everything slowly.

We went inside and Rick began to examine me.

"Does anything hurt worse than yesterday?"

"No. My ribs still hurt the worst."

Brian said, "He's a doctor, Timmy. Tell him about the bathroom."

I asked, "How did you know something was wrong?"

"Because you don't spend thirty minutes in the bathroom."

Rick asked, "Did you have blood in your urine or your poop."

"My pee."

Rick said, "Nothing to worry about. I'll give you a prescription. ." I wondered what kind of medicine works for blood in your pee. Rick continues "No bones were broken, but his ribs were bruised. He just needs time to heal."

Roger and Carlos arrived and Carlos came to check on me. Rick told them it would help if I got in the Jacuzzi.

Carlos and I went outside and got undressed. I looked so pale next to him. With his Puerto Rican heritage, he only went from dark to darker. My summer tan had totally faded. I was small next to him. He had muscular legs and chest—and defined abs—for a kid. He used his height to his advantage. I could tell he liked the way I looked up to him.

I stepped into the pool and got about waist deep before I realized it would hurt too much to swim to the Jacuzzi.

Brian was undressing next to the pool.

Carlos said, "I'll carry you."

Brian said, "No. I'll carry him. You get in the Jacuzzi and I will hand him to you."

It felt good to be so taken care of. I wish life was like this all the time. Brian reached for me with his strong arms and cradled me next to him. He walked carefully to the Jacuzzi. Carlos reached for me and helped me into the hot water. The water felt good on all my sore muscles.

Sensing that I was comparing myself to Carlos, Brian said, "You're perfect Timmy—just the way you are."

"Then why do I get the shit beat out of me everywhere I go?"

"Because they're jealous."

"Jealous of what?"

"Because you are the most beautiful boy around." I knew he was exaggerating, but I liked hearing it anyway.

"Thanks Brian, but I would like to learn to defend myself. I'll work out with you more—anything it takes."

"How about we take karate together?"

"That would be great."

Rick and Todd joined us in the Jacuzzi and I listened to the adults talking. Sometimes the water was too hot and I had to sit on the ledge and cool off.

I kept alternating back and forth. This must have started to effect the men because Brian said, "Nobody touches him."

Then Brian decided it was time for me to get dressed and go in the house for a while. I did as I was told.

CHAPTER EIGHT

THE NEW GIRL

At school on Monday, I was still sore, but things were getting better. The class was loud and everyone was talking about their Christmas break—until everyone stopped talking to look at the new person walk into class. She had long, blond hair and it was straight all the way to her waist. She had clear blue eyes and the daintiest body. She was perfect.

Mr. Gunther walked over to her and introduced her to the class. Jennifer sat in the front row on the other side of the room from me. My desk was next to Brian's and it faced the side of his desk so I could look right at her with no problem. He called the class to order.

"Timmy. Earth to Timmy." The class laughed because I had been staring at her. At recess, I knew I couldn't go out so I stayed inside and helped Brian. The other kids were getting a chance to get to know her and she had a crowd around her. I looked out the window, watching it all.

Brian said, "I think she likes you."

I smiled and said, "I don't think so."

But I sure was day dreaming that she did.

One of the girls slipped me a note that asked if I liked Jennifer. I couldn't stop smiling. I looked up at her and nodded. Brian had seen all this happen and he quickly called the class to order.

After school, I went to Danny's house because I could tell Brian was mad. When I got to Brian's house, we didn't say much to each other and Brian headed to go work out. He knew I was too sore, but he didn't let me off the hook. I did everything he asked. If it wasn't good enough, he yelled, "Come on, wimp, you can do better than that!" Brian had never talked to me this way—and he hardly ever yelled.

"Why are you so mad?"

"Just do your sets." I was fighting the pain and fighting the weights.

I was sweating and so was he. I had worked out with him plenty of times—but not like this. I was on the bench press and I was doing reps six and seven.

He yelled, "Come on!"

I did eight, but nine dropped on my chest.

"You little shit," he yelled. He grabbed me by my pants and picked me up. I grabbed his arms and held tight.

He took me to the bedroom and threw me on the bed. I yelled because it hurt. I was scared and crying. When he stepped back to undress, I made a run for the door. He tripped me and I fell hard. He grabbed my leg and lifted me up. I was dangling in front of him begging and pleading. "Please don't, Brian—not like this." I had never seen that crazy look in his eye.

He stopped when he saw what was happening. He gently put me on the bed. I was crying hysterically because I was scared to death of this side of Brian.

"I am sorry. I am so sorry." I started to calm down. "I'm not going to hurt you. I could never hurt you. You know how much I love you."

The crying stopped, but I still had the hiccups. Little by little, I relaxed until I felt he was a safe place again. I closed my eyes for a few minutes and tried to convince myself that this hadn't happened.

Brian asked, "Are you all right?"

I nodded. I could feel him getting excited. I stayed still, hoping nothing would happen. I was still healing from the beatings and mentally drained from what just happened.

No such luck. Between the anger and the lust, he was going to have his release. When Brian was done, I hurt so badly. I was in hell—mentally and physically—and knew that he did it.

He made me take a shower with him. It made him happy, but I was just glad it was over with. We got out of the shower and dressed.

"Are you still mad at me?"

I shook my head.

Just to make sure, he tickled me gently, being careful of the ribs and offered to cook me anything I wanted to eat. I did my best to put it all behind me quickly so things could get back to normal—whatever normal was.

The next day at school, Brian was exceptionally nice to me. That wasn't unusual. I was his boy. He was always extra nice the day after we had sex.

Danny made sure I was going outside at recess. We liked to play keep away. We played it pretty rough. The girls would sit on the sidelines and talk about us. This made us feel manly. I was still sore, but I did my best to play hard while protecting myself from getting hurt again. I thought I had put on a pretty good show for Jennifer—but I couldn't be sure. It must have worked because she sat next to me at lunch.

It was turning out to be a great day. She was really easy to talk to. We talked all through recess. We walked into class together, laughing and talking. I could see that it had made Brian mad.

During math, Jennifer passed a note to me, but Brian intercepted it. He usually let things like that slide, but he read the note and got mad.

He said, "You have been a disruption since you walked in last week. I am sick of it. This is going to stop." He sent her to the principal's office. She left with tears in her eyes. I felt really sorry for her.

At Brian's, our workout was back to normal. Halfway through, he asked, "Do you like Jennifer?"

"I think I do."

"This isn't good. She's trouble. Stay away from her or I will make it rough on her."

He followed through with his threat. For the rest of the week, he made her cry every day.

On Friday, I wrote her a note. I let Brian read it first and he was satisfied. I told Jennifer that she was really nice, but I just wanted to be friends. I knew I had to do it for her sake, but I could never explain that to her. She cried when she read it. She had not been rejected very often.

Brian had a meeting after school so I went to Danny's house. It was fun sometimes to play games with kids my own age. I wished I had their simple problems.

Brian had gotten permission for me to eat dinner since Roger and Carlos were coming over. As soon as I got there, it was time to start lifting.

Brian asked, "Timmy, why did you like Jennifer?"

"Because she's cute. Why do you like Roger?"

"Oh, that's what this is all about."

"You don't like Roger?"

"I didn't say that."

"Why do you like him?"

"The same reason you like Carlos."

I didn't know where this conversation was going to end up, but I knew it had great possibilities to piss Brian off.

I said, "She's just a friend."

"Do you like Carlos?"

"Yes. But he's just a friend." I could see he was getting mad.

"Do you sleep with your friends?"

"Please, Brian. I only did what I thought you wanted me to do. I always do what I'm supposed to—don't I? I won't do it again. I'll only do what you tell me to. Please don't be mad."

"I'm not mad."

"I'll go home now. I'll leave before they get here … before Carlos gets here."

Brian could see that I was going over the edge. I was babbling and my mind was starting to shut down.

"Timmy, calm down. Everything is going to be okay. Don't worry about Carlos. Let's just go back to working out and forget about everything else. Okay?"

"Brian, can I lie down for a little while?"

"What's the matter?"

"My head hurts really bad."

My head was spinning. I figured he could see anyone he wanted to, but I found it really hard to know the rules to all these games. He got me some aspirin and I went to his room.

It didn't matter if I ever saw any of his friends again. I didn't care if I never saw Carlos again. It was Brian I wanted to please. And if being friends with them made him happy, I could do that. If not talking to Jennifer made him happy, I could do that. I seemed to keep doing the wrong things. I didn't even know how to act anymore. Finally, I fell asleep.

Roger and Carlos came over as planned. Carlos woke me up by tickling my face with a feather.

"Hey sleepyhead, it's time to get up," I just looked at him. "Do you need permission to talk to me?"

I knew that Brian had talked to him.

Carlos asked, "Did you love her?"

"Who? That girl at school? She was just a friend."

"Good, let's go eat."

After having Thai food, it was time for me to leave.

Brian asked, "Timmy, are you okay?"

"Yeah."

"Will I see you tomorrow?"

I nodded.

On my way home, I decided to stay on the sidewalks instead of cutting through the school. It was harder to pedal across the grass. I had to ride past the high school.

When I looked over at the high school, I recognized the guys that had beaten me up. They saw me at the same time and started running toward me. I turned my bike around and pedaled really fast. They were running really fast too. The tallest one almost grabbed my seat, but I barely got away.

"We're really gonna kick your ass now!"

I cut across the grass and pedaled fast and hard all the way home.

On Saturday morning, I rode cautiously to Brian's house. I kept my eyes peeled for those teenagers. The door was locked and the key had been removed. By now I knew the routine. I went to the backyard and waited until I could hear that they were up. I gave them a few minutes and knocked on the front door and Brian let me in. I figured out that Roger and Carlos had spent the night. It felt like I had walked into a secret meeting.

Roger asked if I was hungry. Even though I was, I said no to get back at him.

Brian said, "Timmy, I need to talk to you." I followed him to the bedroom. "I'm fine with you and Carlos, okay? There's nothing to worry about there. Remember you told me that you would do anything for me?" I nodded. "I need you to visit a friend for me. Can you do that?" I nodded again. I didn't really understand what he was asking, but I didn't want Brian angry. "Here's what we'll do. I will take you to his house and drop you off and pick you up later."

He wasted no time and started walking to the car.

"Why can't you stay with me?"

"I just can't. It doesn't work that way."

"Can Carlos come with me?"

"No. He just wants you."

"Do I know him?"

"No."

"Then how can he pick me?"

"He's seen pictures of you."

I was getting really scared. "I don't want to go."

"I know you don't. But this is what I need you to do."

"What do I have to do?"

"Whatever he tells you to." This was the worst news I could hear—and I had experienced a lot.

We pulled up to a mansion. It was brick with white pillars and a circular driveway. The landscape was done to perfection. I wished everything was over. I asked, "Are you mad at me?"

"No."

"Then why are you doing this to me?" In my eyes, this had to be a punishment for something I had done. Brian wouldn't just lend me out to other people.

"Just get out of the car." Brian told me to knock on the door and I did. Brian waited in the car the whole time. The door opened and I was invited in.

There were marble floors in every direction and a wide staircase on the right. The stocky fifty-year-old guy offered me a coke and I accepted. He motioned for me to follow him. We went to an indoor pool and sat on a bench next to each other.

He said, "I've never done this before."

"Me neither."

He told me to stand in front of him and he started to undress me. He told me I was amazing. I was so nervous that I was shaking. Then he undressed. He was really out of shape. He had hair on his chest, arms, back, and neck.

I followed him to a steam room. It was the first time I had ever been in one. He told me to sit across from him and I did.

We sat there for at least fifteen minutes. He watched me in silence, sweat pouring off both of us. I didn't like it at all. It was hard to breathe, but at least it didn't hurt.

He said, "A fantasy come true." He took off his towel. He is fat and sweaty and repulsive. He grabbed me by my head and brought it down to his waist, forcing me to have oral sex with him. It made me sick and I was afraid I was going to gag. I swallowed back the vomit just in time. He only wanted that for a short time. He turned me around and raped me. He showed no mercy. The pain was unbearable and I begged him to stop!

When he was done, we left the steam room and I could finally breathe again. We went to separate showers to clean up. I got dressed, thinking that it was over. I never wanted to have to do anything like that again.

I was wrong—the day had just begun.

He said, "I'm paying a lot for you. I'm not done with you yet."

It was hours until Brian, Roger, and Carlos came to pick me up. I saw the man hand Brian an envelope. That made me mad as hell.

Brian asked, "How did it go?" I looked away. "So you're not going to talk to us." My head didn't move. "He didn't hurt you, did he?"

"Yes, Brian. He did."

"Tell me what happened."

"Why? Neither one of you need the money!"

"It's not about the money. This money is the man paying his dues."

I still didn't get it. "What are dues?"

"So he can be a part of our club."

Carlos said, "I would have taken your place—I really would have—but he picked you."

I tried my best to understand. It was so confusing to a kid my age. All I wanted was Brian in my life—not to be a part of some club or Rick and Todd's toy.

Brian drove us to a really nice restaurant. I wasn't in the mood to act happy, but Carlos kept talking to me and finally made me feel better. It took a while, but I eventually got back to normal—just as I had every other time things turned strange in my life.

CHAPTER NINE

MY BIRTHDAY

Over the last eleven months, I had accumulated a lot of money and gifts. Brian had given me a room in the house just for my stuff. He fixed it up pretty cool. I especially liked my race car set and my stereo. Sometimes the guys just gave me stuff they thought I would like.

At my house, my birthday was no big deal. I had the unfortunate luck for it to always fall near Mother's Day. That was a big deal. Mom would have a party on Sunday to celebrate Mother's Day and invite all her sisters. The cake would always read "Happy Mother's Day" on top and "Happy Birthday" on the bottom.

Mom would have a list with our names and the chores we had to do. I had to clean my room, sweep the sidewalks and patio, and clean the bathroom. When I was done, Mom would inspect. Her mood would determine if it was good enough—no matter how clean it was. She never liked sharing Mother's Day with me and it showed in her attitude.

"Timmy, you call this clean?"

I walked into the bathroom knowing this is a very bad way to start my birthday. She grabbed the back of my neck, dragged me a few steps and pushed my face into the toilet. I tried bracing myself with both hands so my face wouldn't go to the bottom. That pissed her off and she knocked my hands down.

"You think this is clean!"

She pulled my face out of the toilet and I gasped for air. She raised her fists and swung hard four or five times. She put my face back in the toilet and explains in her sick way, "If this was clean, this wouldn't bother you."

She rubbed my face all around the toilet seat. I was crying. She had broken me on my birthday. She let go and I dropped to my knees. She stomped out and I reached for a towel to dry my face off. I cleaned up the mess and hoped it could pass the next inspection.

Mom had three personalities: happy, sad, and really pissed off. Ironically happy and sad would always end up pissed off before the day was over. These personalities were intensified at any family get together. That afternoon, my Mom's sisters and their families came over. We got along well with our cousins Kim and Katrina. They understood our mom because they lived with the same stuff. We never really talked about it. We just understood each other. Dad would barbecue, drink beer, and talk to the guys.

Having Mom's side of the family over was unpredictable and very entertaining. It was great. The four women had so much hate they could start World War III. At any time, an argument could lead to a fistfight. If Grandma showed up, she could really fuel the fire. The kids would sit down and watch the fireworks.

Moms' sisters got into it. Every name in the book was used and I think they made up a few. The worse the language—the better chance of a fight. They loved each other and they loved to argue and fight. In the end, they always made up and acted like nothing was wrong.

When it was time for cake and singing, I was having a good time. Mom handed a piece of cake to everyone. I had opened my gifts—some clothes and a football. I smiled and thanked everyone individually.

Out of the corner of my eye, I could see Mom starting to get mad. I figured her reason was that I hadn't been thankful enough for my presents. She grabbed a piece of cake and the back of my head—and smashed them together.

"You little shit. Why you are so ungrateful? We share Mother's Day with you."

I had cake all over my face and part of my shirt. Everyone looked away from me because they were embarrassed for me. She sent me to my room. I was not surprised, but still humiliated. I spent the rest of my birthday in my room. Being invisible was always better than a beating.

When the guests left, she came to check on me. I wish it had been for the right reason. She came to finish what she had started. Mom swung the broomstick at me and the blow put me on the floor. Once again, I made myself the smallest target possible. She continued ranting and raving about how I had spoiled Mother's Day for her and embarrassed her in front of her family. The hate that could spill out of her was unbelievable. This birthday beating didn't end with a pinch to grow an inch. I cried myself to sleep, wondering what I had done to deserve a mom like her.

I woke up about midnight. I decided to go to Brian's. I knew it was risky, but no one ever checked on me in the middle of the night. I was feeling especially unwanted and would pay any price to get some comfort. The walk was especially scary in the middle of the night. I used all my bravery to ignore the noises that weren't there or see shadows moving toward me.

I opened the door and Brian was watching TV in the living room.

"What are you doing here in the middle of the night?"

I broke down and cried. He held me and made me feel safe. I finally got the story out.

He held me tight to his chest and said, "Next weekend, you are going to get the best birthday party ever! You don't have to share it with anyone! And it will be just a special day for you." He pulled me up on his lap to watch TV with him. I must have fallen into a deep sleep because I didn't even feel him move me to the bed.

In the morning, Brian was looking at me. I gave him a big smile.

He said, "You probably should go home before they notice you are gone."

"It's okay. They will think I just got up early and left for school."

I was thinking ahead to the summer and knew it was going to be great because I could spend the days at Brian's house. We would have a lot more time together that didn't include his friends. I was sad that he wouldn't be my teacher for fourth grade, but the confidence he helped instill in me would make it easier.

I arrived as early as I could on Saturday morning—maybe a little too early because it was still dark. Brian had teased me all week about what a great surprise was in store for me. I was excited to feel so important to someone. I let myself in and went to my room to play so Brian could sleep later.

The minutes passed like hours. I finally went in and jumped on the bed. Brian laughed and tickled me. He looked at the clock and tried to act mad, but couldn't do it. He gave me ten spanks on the butt and said, "Guess what your surprise is."

"What? You have to tell me!"

"You're going to Disneyland today!"

I had never been there and yelled, "No way! This is great!"

Brian explained that some of our friends were going with us. I had mixed feelings because I really cherished our time alone. I was really glad to hear that Carlos would be there too. He had bought me a really cool outfit to wear that day and I changed into it. We met the rest of the guys at Denny's for breakfast.

Brian was right—everyone did their best to make it a special day for me. One of the guys was an executive for Disneyland we got the VIP treatment all day. I didn't have to wait in any lines. If I was too short, they still let me on the ride. The guys with us would fight over who would ride with me on the next ride. I really was king for a day.

We ate lunch at the Pirates of the Caribbean Restaurant, which was also one of my favorite rides. I also like the haunted house and the log ride. I was pretty sure we went on every ride in the park—and some twice. The other guys left about an hour earlier than we did.

On the way home, I kept thanking him, telling him that it had been the very best birthday ever.

I thought the day would be over when we pulled into the driveway, but Brian still had one more surprise waiting for me.

When I walked in, everyone yelled, "Happy birthday, Timmy!"

It was great! Everyone was there. The kids decided to go swimming and the adults did the cooking. There was a huge birthday cake and a table full of presents.

I didn't know if anything was going to be expected of us—and it must have showed on my face.

Carlos said, "Don't worry—nothing is going to happen tonight. This is your birthday. That's all."

After swimming, we ate and then it was time to open my presents. The guys went all out and got me really great gifts. I got a cool stereo, an expensive remote control car, and some really cool clothes. I thanked them all for what they had done for me.

Brian's gift was the best. It was a karate outfit. I looked at him a little unsure about what it meant.

Brian smiled and said, "I'm tired of you getting the shit beat out of you. I signed us both up for karate lessons." Knowing he was going to be there with me made it even better. It was the best gift any kid could ask for. I ran and gave him a big hug and kiss.

On Monday, the kids were excited because we got the next week off of school and we were counting the days until then.

On the way to Brian's house, Rick pulled up next to me and said, "Get in."

I panicked and said, "Brian is expecting me."

"Tell him you met up with your brother and had to go home. Now get in!"

This wasn't the nice Rick that had hung out with us at Disneyland. This wasn't the Rick that was one of Brian's best friends. This was the Rick that scared the shit out of me and I couldn't tell anyone what was happening. I was nervous as hell all the way to the house. Anxiety was mounting with each mile that took us closer. I couldn't even imagine what they had planned for me this time.

Todd was waiting for us in the driveway. He opened my door, grabbed my arm, and pulled me out. I said, "Stop. You know I'm not going to run."

"You'll do as I say!" He slapped me upside the head. He was strong and it hurt. I tried to pull away, but that made it worse. He pulled me back and slapped my face. I couldn't understand why things had to start out like this. What pleasure did they get out of the violence? I would have run away if I knew what was in store for me.

Todd pushed me to the ground and put handcuffs on me. This was turning really strange really fast. He stood me up to walk into the house. I was scared enough to start crying.

At the door, he stopped and told me to take my shoes off. I couldn't believe that it even mattered. We went through the laundry room and into the garage. I couldn't believe what I saw. They had turned the garage into a House of Pain. There was a balance beam held up by two drums and a piece on the floor to tie down my feet. A movie camera was on a tripod and a table held whips and chains and other unimaginable things.

Todd left the room for a minute and I started backing up. I ran into Rick and cried, "Please, Rick, you can't do this. You've got to help me. This is crazy."

He was not hearing a word of it; his mind was already made up.

"You're going to be all right. Now move over there." He pointed to the beam and I froze. He pushed me over there. I stumbled and he decided to take the handcuffs off of me. I was begging for my life the whole time. He took off my shirt and shackled my hands down. He took off the rest of my clothes and did the same to my feet.

Todd was dressed like a biker from hell and wore a leather mask. It took a second to realize that another person had walked in dressed the same way. I was not sure who was Todd and who was the stranger. That made it even worse. One of them grabbed a leather whip and started to hit my butt. He didn't do it very hard, but it was still scary.

After few soft hits, he hit the inside my leg hard and it startled me. All over my body, they hit me soft and then hard. It was starting to hurt and burn all over. Rick was at the camera, making sure he didn't miss anything.

The fear mixed with pain was getting unbearable. The way I was strapped down made it hard to hold my body up. I pulled against the straps and yelled. No one cared—they probably liked it. My strength finally gave out and I tried to use the beam to hold me up. One of the men walked in front of me, hitting a nightstick against the palm of his hand. I thought he was going to beat me.

Between the sweat and the tears, I could barely see. The guy wiped my face and eyes so I wouldn't miss anything. The other guy went behind me and started to have sex with me. The guy in front of me made a circle with his fingers and ran the stick in and out. Even at ten, I knew what that meant. I began screaming, yelling uncontrollably, and pulling against the straps. Rick stopped filming and walked over to me. I just collapsed. My arms and legs went limp and I passed out.

When I woke up in the living room, Rick and Todd were standing over me. I must have kept crying because I came out of it sobbing.

Todd yelled, "Timmy, calm down!" I couldn't help it. "If you don't stop, I'm going to beat the hell out of you." I cried even harder.

Rick said, "Timmy, it's okay. Nothing else is going to happen. No one is going to hurt you." I took a deep breath. "What's wrong with you? Have we ever hurt you before?"

I wanted to answer that truthfully, but I knew they wouldn't believe me. I just stared at him, not answering.

Rick took me to the bathroom to clean me up. "Timmy, what did you think we were going to do?"

"I don't know. It was really scary. Who is that other guy?"

"That is none of your business. Is that why you freaked out?"

Nodding seemed to be the easiest answer. Rick started the bath for me and put bubbles in the water. I got in and it felt good.

I said, "Todd scares me."

Rick joined me in the tub.

"Don't be afraid of Todd."

"He doesn't like me."

"Yes, he does. He just doesn't communicate very well." That outfit communicated a lot to me. He rubbed my feet and it tickled. "Will it make you feel better if Todd talks to you?"

I shrug my shoulders knowing it would take a lot more than that. "I wish you would tell me what you are going to do. The stuff you do freaks me out."

"Why is it any different than the parties? You don't know what's going to happen and you don't freak out there."

"That's because I'm not the only boy there—and Brian is there too."

"So it would make a difference if we talked to you?"

I nodded. I didn't know what to say. I wanted to say it would be really great if they just left me alone.

I was too scared to speak my mind to adults. I had never told my mom to stop beating me or my brother. I had never told Brian that I wouldn't go to the parties. I never told Rick and Todd that they couldn't use me anymore. I wished I was bigger and stronger. I wished life had been different.

Rick got out of the tub and left. I got out and looked in the mirror. To my surprise, there were no welts. My skin was red, but I could tell it would fade. I didn't have my clothes so I put a towel around my waist and walked to the kitchen. Rick and Todd were talking, but they stopped when I walked in.

Todd said, "I'm sorry for being so rough."

Rick asked, "So, are you okay now?" I nodded. "Are you sure?"

I took a deep breath and said, "Yes."

I thought they would let me get dressed and take me home, but they had other ideas. They told me they wanted to finish the movie.

Rick said, "We'll tell you everything we are going to do." I was amazed that they would do that to me. "Don't worry. We won't hurt you." Why do I keep hearing that so much? Rick put his arm around me and walked me back to the garage.

On Friday, the kids were excited; for the first time, I was also. I stayed to help Brian clean up the room and told him that my mom wanted me to come home right after school. I would come over later if it worked out. He told me we would go to the beach the next day. I was really excited about that.

As I walked home, I reflected on the past year. I couldn't imagine life without Brian. I felt like he had saved me. Other kids wanted to hang out with me. When things were crazy at home, I knew where I could feel safe and secure and loved.

At the front door, I could hear my brother getting his ass kicked. I was too scared to open it, but I wanted to get it over with so I could go to Brian's. After most beatings, Mom would be in a better mood—just in time for Dad to walk in the door and get the best side of her. I think beating us was a stress reliever for her. I started down the hall. I knew she was near but didn't know where she was hiding. She jumped out of the closet and hit me with the broomstick. I fell to the ground.

"No, Mom. No." Since she loved to hear us beg for mercy, I started right away.

"Didn't I tell you to come home right after school?" *A lot of good that did my brother.*

I crawled toward my room while she hit my back and legs. She was getting a lot of swings in and I was crying and screaming. She stopped and I gasped for air between hits. I looked up and was amazed at the hate and rage on her face. She was repositioning herself so she could get to my stomach. It shocked the hell out of me! She knocked the air out of me and I knew I couldn't take another shot like that. I quickly rolled away from her. She took her time working over my backside. She would hit whatever was available. If I blocked high, she hit low. Finally she left; I guess her arms got tired. I was just thankful it was over.

As I was trying to catch my breath, I rolled onto my back. When she came back in, I was surprised that she stabbed me in the stomach with the broomstick. I rolled into a ball again. She kept using the end of the stick and stabbing at my stomach and ribs, anything she could reach. The whole time she was yelling that I hadn't done what I had been told. Luckily someone knocked on our front door and she had to go see who it was. I was praying that it was over with. I crawled to my bed and got under the covers. I cried hard; her rage was worse than usual. The summer was starting out badly.

I daydreamed about Brian being my dad and how great my life would be with just the two of us. I thought about it so hard that when I did fall asleep I kept dreaming about a new, happy life. I woke up and it was dark outside. I could hear Mom and Dad talking. I figured my brother was curled up on his bed too. I started to get up, but the pain was so bad I just laid back down. It just wasn't worth it.

I fell back to sleep and woke up again at two o'clock. I knew Brian wouldn't be up, but I had to get somewhere safe to heal for a while. I moved slowly and quietly. I rode my bike—even though it hurt to pedal, it was faster and less effort than walking. Roger's car was in the driveway. I figured the key probably wouldn't be there. To my surprise, it was, and I let myself in. Brian's bedroom door was shut and I saw Carlos in the guest room. I curled up on the couch and turned the TV on low. Mom must have sucked the life out of me because I fell asleep again.

I woke to Carlos tickling my face with a piece of string. He asked how long had I been there. I told him not long. He playfully jumped on me wanting to wrestle. I screamed in pain.

He jumped off and asked, "What's wrong?" He tried to lift my shirt, but I kept a tight hold on it. He persisted and I slowly gave in.

Carlos went to get Brian. Brian gently pulled me up and helped me take off my shirt. He stared at my chest, stomach, and back. "That bitch!" There were so many bruises it was hard to find skin. "Those are your clothes from yesterday, aren't they?"

I nodded. He pushed gently on my ribs and determined they were not broken.

He took me through the bedroom and Roger was still in bed. Brian turned on the shower and helped me wash my hair and my body. He was extra gentle, but it still hurt. I dried myself off because it was easier. He let me wear one of his shirts—I always felt special when I got to wear one. I could tell he was very upset this time. I left for the kitchen while he was finishing in the shower.

Carlos was cooking and it smelled really good. He asked, "Do you want an omelet?"

"What's that?"

"You've never had one? They're really good. I will make you a special one." I smiled. Carlos always took good care of me. "So what happened? What did you do?"

"Nothing"

"Really? Nothing?"

"I walked in from school and she was waiting for me."

"You're kidding."

"She was hiding in the closet."

"No way. Your mom isn't right!"

"Where's your mom?"

"In Puerto Rico."

"Did she beat you?"

"No. My mom is great. But Dad sure could be mean. Mom sent me to live with Roger."

"Are you happy?"

"Yeah."

"Did Roger adopt you?"

"No."

"I wish I could live here with Brian."

Carlos put his arm around me. It hurt, but I didn't say anything. I let him comfort me. Roger walked in and asked what was burning. Carlos told him it was my omelet.

I was so hungry it still tasted great.

Roger sat down and said, "Timmy, let me see your mother's handiwork."

He lifted up my shirt. That was all I had on. A year earlier, I would have died of embarrassment but today it was the least of my worries.

Roger said, "Not too bad."

Carlos said, "Not if you're a punching bag."

I smiled at Carlos as I put the shirt back on. Brian walked in and announced that we weren't going to the beach.

Carlos asked, "Why not?"

Brian pointed at me.

I said, "I'll keep my shirt on and no one will know."

Brian asked, "What about all the bruises on your legs?"

"You guys just go without me. Don't stay just for me."

Carlos said, "No way. It won't be the same without you. What's wrong, Timmy?"

"I don't want to be the reason you don't go."

Brian said, "You're not the reason. Your mother is. The weather is nice so we'll stay here and go in the pool. I'll call Hank and Nick and see if they can come over. We'll just have a pool party."

That was the first time that I had heard the name of Nick's dad. Usually the guys just had faces and no names at the parties. I still wasn't sure what I thought about Nick. Sometimes I thought he liked me, but other times, I thought he didn't.

They showed up a little while later. Carlos was the oldest—and definitely was the leader of the kid group. I liked it that way because he was always good to me and looked out for me. Nick was almost as tall as Carlos, but he was slender. He could be bossy, but Carlos had real leadership qualities.

We decided to go swimming and I slowly got in the pool.

Nick said, "Come on, you wimp. It's not that bad."

Nick had the bright idea to play Marco Polo and made me Marco on the day I couldn't swim. I did my best to play and keep my mind off other things. Nick led me to the deep end a few times. Carlos always played fair and that made it fun.

In the shallow end, I tagged Nick and he called me a cheater. He picked me up by my sides and threw me in the deep end. Carlos told him to stop. I made it to the ledge, but I was crying.

"Suck it up, you big baby."

When it was Nick's turn to be Marco, he was mad. Carlos found it easy to stay away from him, but I was moving slower than ever. Nick tagged me and then jumped on me with his full weight. I start to go under the water. I was gasping for air until I went under. He stayed on top of me and I felt like he really wanted to hurt me.

Suddenly he moved off my chest and I came up, gasping for air. My stomach and ribs were killing me. I climbed out of the water and caught my breath. Nick jumped up and ran into the house. Carlos had come from the deep end and punched him in the face.

A few minutes later, the men came out of the house.

Roger asked, "What the hell is going on?"

Carlos said, "Nick has been picking on Timmy and trying to hurt him ever since we started swimming."

Hank asked, "Is this true?"

I nodded. Hank stormed into the house after Nick. Roger and

Brian got in the pool for a while and I relaxed in the sun. I closed my eyes, but it felt like the world was spinning.

The guys were playing in the pool. I reflected on how complicated my life was. My home life sucked because I was always trying to avoid Mom's rage. I was juggling two lives and trying to keep them separate. It wasn't easy. It seemed I had a face that you either loved or hated. Brian made me feel loved and needed. I felt accepted for the first time in my life, but there was pain in his world too. I guess there was always a price to pay. I felt a shadow fall across my face.

"Timmy, Nick has something to say to you," Hank said.

"I'm sorry," Nick said.

After I accepted his apology, Nick surprised me by lying down next to me. He said, "I was mad at you."

"Why?"

"I used to be everyone's favorite until you came along. Now they like you best."

"I don't think that's true."

"It is. But it's not your fault. I think they always like the youngest one best. I'm sorry. I'd like to be your friend. We kids got to stick together."

I smiled and he went to talk to Carlos. He jumped in the pool and they talked and worked it out.

I watched them get a volleyball game together. All I could do was keep score. I got sleepy and took a nap. They woke me up for lunch and I put on my shirt and went inside.

Nick said, "There's a big party in two weeks."

I tried to hide my nervousness. Carlos and Nick always liked making money and acting, but I still wasn't comfortable with it. I was afraid of making a mistake or looking stupid or worse, getting a beating. It was hard to have all those guys watching my every move for hours on end. Our job was to give them a show. To me, it was like being naked in public—but no one was shocked that I was naked.

CHAPTER TEN

THE THREE CROSSES

Time went by fast, and soon it was time for another party. I went to Brian's early that morning and crawled into his bed. Those were my favorite times when I felt safe and loved and secure.

We showered and I had a definite effect on him. We rinsed off and he led me to the bed. I knew what he liked best and what worked best for me where it didn't hurt so badly. But most of all I wanted to make him happy. When it was over, I listened to his heart pounding. I wanted to ask him if we could miss the party, but I knew that would only make him mad. I already knew the answer to that question.

We went to breakfast and people assumed I was his son. I really loved that and played up to it whenever I could. We ran errands and soon it was time to go to the party.

On the way, Brian told me to be strong and to do whatever I was told. *This can't be good.* He reminded me how much money I would make. The money never meant anything to me. I got everything I wanted from having Brian in my life.

We pulled up to a huge double gate with an intercom. We were let in and I saw the largest, fanciest house I had ever seen. There were already ten or eleven cars there and I figured we were the last to arrive. A big man let us in and we walked across marble floors into a giant living room. The house was two stories tall and had huge front doors that opened wide. There was a chandelier in the entranceway that sparkled and a huge staircase on one side.

Carlos and Nick excitedly showed me around. We went down a long hallway to a huge playroom with a pool table, arcade games, and a bowling alley. We played there until the men came and got us. I thought they were going to have us start by swimming, but they took us to a dressing room and handed us leather loincloths. I had no idea how to put it on.

Nick said, "Carlos, what happened to you?"

Carlos had pubic hair, but Nick and I were still too young.

Carlos said, "Roger made me shave. He says I look younger this way." Carlos put the loincloth on right the first time and had to help us put ours on.

I asked, "Aren't we going swimming?"

They just shook their heads and looked at me like my young age was really showing. I was still hoping we wouldn't have to do anything too freaky or painful—but this wasn't a good start.

Hank and Roger were waiting for us outside the dressing room. They looked us over to see if we were dressed right.

Brian said, "You guys ready?"

We nodded and the men led us out. We went out into the backyard, which was a few acres. There were more men than usual—I counted sixteen. I couldn't believe my eyes. They were walking us up to three crosses! Someone had made them with posts and cemented them inside a big tire. They put Carlos in the middle and tied his wrists down with leather straps and strapped his feet at the bottom. I didn't know what to think. I sure was glad they didn't go for real nails.

Nick was still tall enough to stand and reach the crossbeam. When it was my turn, I quickly realized how being short was going to hurt. I had to stand on my tiptoes for them to strap my wrists. I would have to stay that way .It was so hard to take a breath. I thought someone would raise the step my feet were on, but nobody did.

Something made me look up since I was facing the house. I could see an outline in the upstairs window. I looked harder and could tell someone was watching us from that window. This was creepy to me—for some reason, it embarrassed me more than I already was.

The men stood back to look at their handiwork—and I couldn't believe what the evening was turning into. A man started taking pictures, some were individual shots and others were all three of us. I could hear the excitement in their voices as they played out this fantasy. I could see the lust in their eyes. A man walked up to me and I couldn't believe my bad luck. It was the man I had sat with in the steam room. He kissed me and whispered, "You are so beautiful."

He took off my loincloth and left me naked on the cross. I was trying not to squirm, but I was still standing on my toes to breathe.

Roger walked over to Carlos and took off his leather wrap and then Nick's. I was surprised because both of the boys were physically excited—nothing about this night made me feel that way. This caused more excitement and more picture taking. I was glad the attention was off me for a while. Brian could see how hard it was to stand and he came and nailed another board a couple of inches higher for me. I could finally stand and breathe easier. The men stood around talking to each other about what they were going to do to us later. Since it was too early to start with us, they started the night's other activities.

The men decided to swim, play volleyball, and eat dinner. We stayed strapped to the stupid crosses and it entertained them to know we were stuck there.

Carlos said, "Nick, how are you doing?"

"The wood is hurting the heels of my feet."

Carlos said, "Yeah, mine are killing me too. Timmy, how are you holding up?"

It was still hard to talk and he heard the panic in my voice, "I'm okay, Carlos."

"Just calm down. It's just a game. You'll be all right."

Carlos asked for Roger to come over. "I don't know how much longer we can take this."

Roger said, "You don't have a choice now, do you?"

He walked off. The men talked to each other and watched us as they finished eating.

Nick said, "I don't care what they do to me—as long as they take me off this cross."

Carlos asked, "What if they never let us get down?"

Nick said, "I guess we just die here."

I was starting to panic again. I thought about how no one knew where I was. How would anyone ever find me? Carlos realized I was taking them seriously and said, "We're just kidding, Timmy, calm down."

The men were already done eating and started gathering around us. Carlos was approached first. A man grabbed his privates and he flinched. This made the guy smile. He ended up having oral sex with Carlos as we all watched. Then they took him off his cross. A man started to kiss Nick and then he performed oral sex with Nick as everyone watched—and then they took him off his cross.

A guy name Bill started to kiss my face and chest and tried to perform oral sex on me. I was too nervous and in too much pain and discomfort for that. My body wasn't reacting at all.

He said, "You can't come down until you get off."

I had been around this group long enough to know what that meant. Bill kept trying different things, but my arms, legs, and back hurt so much it didn't matter. I looked up at the window again at the person watching us; it looked like a girl because of the long hair. She was staring intently at me. I was completely at the mercy of all these men, but having this girl watching totally broke me.

Finally, they decided to let me hang up there for a few more hours—and then I'd play by their rules. Then they all walked away.

I yelled and begged for mercy, but they all went into the house. I started to cry, but no one could hear me. I looked up at the window again and noticed the girl was watching through a pair of binoculars. It made me feel better to think I wasn't alone. I was up there for what seemed like hours. The pain was excruciating.

I screamed really loud and started to cry uncontrollably. Brian finally walked over to me and told me to relax. I looked away from him. He told me to look at him, but I was really losing it. I was so scared that my mind started spinning. My body started to shake and everything went black.

I woke up tired and out of it at Brian's house.

I said, "I'm sorry. Please don't be mad."

"No, Timmy. I should be sorry. Will you forgive me?"

I felt really weak, but I said I would.

Brian said, "Good, let's get you cleaned up."

He carried me to the bathroom. I couldn't even remember the last time my own father had picked me up. He already had the bath running as he lowered me into the tub. Then he got in and started washing the sweat and dirt off me.

"Are you sure you're not mad at me?"

I thought I would be the one in lot of trouble for ruining the party. I smiled at him and shook my head.

"Timmy, you amaze me."

I didn't understand, but it was nice to hear. There was a knock at the door. Brian got out, put on a robe, and answered the front door.

There was a lot of yelling, but I could tell Brian wasn't backing down. I smiled in hopes that maybe this would put an end to all the parties for me. I doubted it, but I could at least hope. He came back in and got back into the tub.

He said, "Timmy, do you know how special you are? You are young and beautiful. Hell, after what just happened, you are the only reason I wasn't kicked out of the group."

I smiled, but I wasn't sure how to take that. I said, "They have Carlos and Nick. Why am I so important?"

"They will settle for Carlos and Nick, but they really want you."

"But Carlos and Nick look great."

I knew this counted for a lot in life. Before I met Brian, I had thought I was an ugly kid. People always wanted to beat me up. I always felt like the redheaded stepchild that no one wanted. I figured I had a face that only a mother could love—except that one didn't work in my life either. I felt like I wasn't cute, smart, or strong. Little by little, Brian had given me confidence in all those areas. I felt loved by him and he broke me out of the shell I was living in. He made me popular and gave me a place to hide from my mom. He had become my life—at least the good part of it.

"Trust me, Timmy. It is you they want."

I had no idea that it was the younger, the better for these guys. I was just glad that I was staying the night at Brian's and the party could now just be a bad memory.

"At nine o'clock, Roger and Carlos came over to the house. Brian and I were cuddled on the couch watching TV. Brian got up and he and Roger went to the bedroom to talk.

I said, "Are they mad at me?"

Carlos said, "Not you. They're mad at Brian, they think he overreacted."

"What are they going to do?"

Carlos laughed and said, "Shit, nothing! Brian always has the best-looking boys."

"What do you mean by that?"

"Hell, Timmy, he's a schoolteacher. He can pick from the cream of the crop. I heard the guys say that you are the best one so far."

I knew this was supposed to be a compliment, but it scared me. I asked, "Even after tonight?"

"Hell yes. Especially after tonight. People always want what they can't have and tonight they couldn't have you. Guess how much we got paid?"

"How much?" I didn't care if I got any money.

"Nick and I got $1,000 apiece."

No way! That's a lot of money, but you two sure did earn it. Carlos, what are you going to do with your money?"

"I'm saving for a car."

I didn't see Brian for the rest of the night. Carlos and I fell asleep on the couch. I woke up to breakfast being cooked.

At my house, there wasn't much of a schedule. Dad was going out of town more and more to work and Mom would sleep more and more. She didn't cook nearly as much and cleaned only what she had to. She could be a lot more fun too; sometimes we would go to the movies and get ice cream. I never let my guard down because it could also mean we were beaten more often and more severely because Dad wasn't around to see it. She never had to explain her actions to him, but it kept her in check at times. He was her sanity in her insane world.

The rest of the weekend went smoothly. I liked that nothing was expected of me. The guys took us to the beach and we played hard and came home. I got home to find Mom in a good mood and went to bed more relaxed than usual.

About three weeks into the summer, my brother woke me on a Monday morning and told me I had a phone call. Rick told me to meet him at the school in thirty minutes.

"I can't." I would say anything to get out of going with him.

Rick said, "Timmy, if you don't meet me, I'll tell your mother everything you are doing. If you don't believe me, just put her on the phone right now."

There went any argument I could think of. I said, "I'll be there."

Tom asked, "Who was that on the phone?"

"Just a friend's dad whose planning a surprise party for his son and I was invited." Luckily that satisfied his curiosity.

I got dressed and walked to school. I felt like a dead man walking. If only I was, then at least I would know how this story ended. But the unknown was a lot worse. Rick was waiting and yelled, "Get in the car." I did. "Don't ever tell me you can't come over!" I nodded because he had made his point earlier. I realized I hadn't eaten anything and that was making my stomach feel even worse.

I asked, "Can I get some breakfast? I left the house without eating anything." He told me he would cook me some eggs at his house.

We pulled into his driveway and thankfully Todd wasn't there grabbing and throwing me around like last time. We went in the front door and I could hear Todd talking to Hank. Rick told me to sit at the table while the three men talked.

Hank sat down next to me and said, "So, Timmy, I hear you're good at keeping secrets."

All the men laughed. I didn't even answer. I really wanted to run for the door and get away from all of them. I worked at staying calm. Nick could see my panic and told me everything will be all right. It was nice to have a friend at a time like that.

As we ate, I listened to the conversation and put the story together. Hank found out about the movie and wanted in on it. Nick even seemed excited about it. I figured he wasn't listening very well to what was going to happen in the making of the movie. Nick asked if we could go swimming while they made plans for our day.

We swam for a while and made our way to the Jacuzzi. I asked Nick what was going on. I wanted his take on all that was happening; maybe he could fill in the blanks.

"We are going to make some money today. We are going to make the rich doctors happy and I get to spend the day with you."

"I didn't think you really liked me." This was important today because he may be the only friend I had.

"I do. Rick and Todd can be really mean sometimes, but don't worry, I'm here. What happened last time? They said you really freaked out."

"They tried to scare me and it worked." He kept waiting for more details so I finally told him the whole story. Rick told us it was time to get started. Nick was excited for this adventure. I was moving a lot slower than he was. I couldn't figure out why he was so excited, but I would get my answer a little later. Nothing bothered Nick—nothing was too disgusting or creepy—and he wasn't bashful or ashamed. When it came to anything sexual, he was nonchalant. It was all about the money and he would do anything to get it. I guess he had learned how to shut down and perform.

Rick led us to the garage and they had made a lot of changes since the last time. It looked more like a movie set, but the theme was the same. Nick seemed to love it and I just wanted it over with. We got dressed and fixed our hair. Then they gave us our instructions.

I had to walk over to the beam and act like I was nervous. *No problem there.* I didn't even have to act. Nick walked over and slowly undressed me and I did the same to him. I was strapped down on the beam. Nick picked up a whip and beat the hell out of me while I screamed, cried, and begged him to stop. There was no acting involved—then he kissed me and raped me. It was pure torture. Todd came in wearing a mask and pushed Nick off me. He slapped Nick just as it had been planned.

Todd acted like he was raping Nick. Nick was yelling and screaming like he was in pain. It was convincing enough that I didn't know if he was acting or not. Todd unbuckled me from the beam and put Nick on it. I was supposed to whip him and get behind him to finish off the scene. They called it quits after that. I unbuckled Nick and he looked all sad and hurt.

I asked, "Hey, are you all right?"

"Hell yeah, I'm just playing my part."

Since that part of the day was over, we headed back to the pool. Nick treated me like I was his best friend. We played for an hour or so until Hank told Nick it was time to go. After they left, I asked Todd, "Who's going to take me home?"

"What's your hurry? Got something to do?"

I shrugged. I was thinking that anywhere was better than staying here, but I didn't want to make him mad. He playfully tossed me in the deep end and then jumped in.

He came up behind me and dunked me. I pushed away and floated to the top for air. He followed me and acted like it was a game and got a better hold on me and pushed me under again. I had time to realize what he was going to do and gulped some air. This time, he held me longer and I was using all my strength and kicking to get to the top.

Finally, he let up and I gasped for air, wondering what the heck was going on. I swam away and he followed. I started to panic and tried to talk to him. He ignored me and put me under one more time—just a little longer. I knew I couldn't keep doing this so when he let me up, I grabbed his neck with all my strength and wouldn't let go. He tried to push me off, but I was holding tight. I was crying and scared to death. He walked to the shallow end and told me to let go of his neck when we get to the steps. I did because I finally felt safe.

"You are such a big baby! Why don't you toughen up?"

I couldn't believe his stupidity. I asked, "Why do you like hurting kids?"

He said, "Not all kids. Just you."

I knew it was time to get away from this guy. Rick came walking up and he could see that I'd been crying. "Timmy, what's wrong?"

"He was holding me under the water."

"Grow up," He said to Todd.

Todd just laughed it off like it was nothing and offered to fix lunch. I was glad I would at least be away from him.

Since Rick and I had talked a couple of weeks ago, I felt like he was more of a friend. He let me do flips off his shoulders and we swam for a while. He came up behind me and started kissing my neck. I knew where it was leading. He was the guy behind the camera today and probably had felt left out. When he was done, he asked me if I wanted to watch the movie. I was thinking, no way, but maybe nothing else would happen if I played along.

Todd had lunch ready and we all ate. Then they took me to a room where the windows had been blacked out and there were some couches. They started the projector and I found it really hard to watch myself being molested. The expression on my face pretty much represented what I had been feeling at the time. The whole thing appalled and disgusted me and it was brutal. I acted nonchalant because it was expected of me. I hoped they would be finished with me, but the movie had an effect on them and we had to go back to the garage one more time. After that, they finally took me back to school so I could go home.

I felt so violated and defeated. I didn't know how many people would see that film. Everyone's face was covered but mine and Nick's. Nick's attitude was that he was a great actor now and every role he played was practice for Hollywood. I couldn't bear the thought of anyone watching that horrible film. What if Brian saw it? He would be so disappointed in me. Hell, what would my parents think? I had to block it out or I would go crazy.

CHAPTER ELEVEN

THE NEW KID

Brian and I had a summer schedule. We worked out almost every day unless my mom had me doing something else—or Rick and Todd summoned me. The strange part of all those secrets was keeping them straight. Brian thought my mom had me busy when Rick and Todd made me come over. Mom thought I had a bunch of different friends that I spent time with.

Brian and I had been going to karate on Tuesday and Thursday nights and I was getting pretty good at it. The teacher told Brian he was a natural. It was fun because we would test for our new belts at the same time and move up together. Between Brian and karate, it was really helping my confidence and helped me defend myself from other kids.

One day on my way to Brian's house, I was passing a group of kids that I usually got along with. One of the big kids reached out and knocked me off my bike. I was surprised because I hadn't had any problems with him before. I got to my feet quickly and put up my hands. He was laughing at me and then I kicked him right in the nuts. He fell to the ground crying and holding his balls like they were going to fall off. I got on my bike and rode like crazy to tell Brian the good news.

I dropped my bike on the porch and ran into the house to tell him what just happened. He was talking to Richard, I recognized him from the parties. He had brown hair, a beard and mustache and was overweight but solid. They stopped talking to listen to me and congratulated me. Brian told me there was a guest in my room I should go meet.

I looked in my room. I could hear him playing with my race cars. His back was to me and he had long brown hair past his shoulders. It looked like a girl from the back. I said hi and it startled him.

He said, "They said I could play in here."

I told him that it was okay. Troy looked like a model. He was a little taller than me and had an athletic build. His long brown hair was highlighted from the sun. His face was pure innocence and his smile was the kind no one could resist. He had big, beautiful brown eyes. I sat next to him and joined in playing with the race cars. I was trying to figure him out.

"How old are you?"

"I'm twelve and you're ten." *Like this gives him an advantage.*

"How do you know Richard?"

"He's my stepdad. My real dad doesn't have anything to do with me. Richard married my mom when I was five." I figured that maybe he wasn't a part of all this craziness.

We played and laughed and started to relax. Troy was a normal kid. He looked around my room and told me it was cool. I liked hearing that.

"Who is Brian to you?"

"My teacher."

"You live with your teacher?"

"No. I'm just here a lot."

"Do you get to swim in the pool?"

"Yeah."

"And he buys you all these toys?"

"Yeah"

"Wow. I wish he was my teacher."

Brian called for me to come to the living room. "How do you like Troy?"

"I like him."

"We need to teach him the ropes."

"Why?"

"They want to hang out with our group."

"What do you want me to do?"

"Both you guys go swimming with no suits." I was uneasy in this role. I didn't feel like a leader and I didn't want to see any more kids get pulled into my world. I walked back to the bedroom and asked Troy if he wanted to go swimming.

"Yeah. But I didn't bring any swimming trunks."

"Don't worry. We're both boys. Let's go."

We walked outside and he had a funny look on his face. I just undressed and jumped in. He stood there unsure of what to do.

"Hurry up. The water feels great."

"I don't think I want to swim." I kept encouraging him. Finally I swam to the edge and splashed him a little. Richard and Brian came out; they had been watching from the window.

Richard asked, "What's wrong, Troy?"

"I don't have a swimsuit."

"We're all guys. It's no big deal. Go on." Troy slowly undressed and jumped in.

We had fun playing games and swimming for a while. When Brian and Richard joined us, Troy got bashful and swam to a corner. I went over to Brian and he grabbed me by the waist and threw me into the air. It was great. We did that a couple of times and then he started letting me do flips. Troy was looking and wanting to join in. Brian whispered to me to ask him to join us. I did and he swam right to Brian. I went to Richard and the men took turns throwing us. We cheered loud for each other.

We tired the men out after an hour. While they were getting out of the pool, Richard stopped and whispered something in Troy's ear.

He looked at me and said, "Teach him."

I wasn't quite sure what they meant so I went to Brian and asked him.

He said, "Do what Carlos has shown you."

"Does he know what this is about?"

"That's why he is here. He wants to." I wished they had taken him to Carlos.

I walked back to the shallow end where Troy was standing and asked, "Do you know what they want us to do?"

"Yeah."

"And you're okay with it?" He nodded. "Have you done it before?"

"Yeah, with Richard, but he wants me to know more." *You have no idea. If you join this group, your life will never be the same.* I had no idea how I was going to go about this project.

We walked through the living room. I was leading him to my room and Brian asked, "Where are you guys going?"

"My room."

"No. You guys stay right here where we can see you." You would think I would be surprised or appalled, but I had been through too much by then.

Troy said, "Not me. Not now."

I turned to face Troy and told him to relax. I said it with authority and it surprised even me. "This is what you came for, right?" He nodded. I told him to forget about everybody else. Then his lesson began.

When it was done, we headed back to the pool as if it never happened. We looked at each other and laughed and played like young boys again. He had a way about him that reminded me of Danny. I could feel like a normal kid around him even after what had just happened.

The next day, Roger and Carlos went with us to the beach. Richard and Troy were going to meet us there. Brian played a while with me in the waves and got tired. I never got tired of playing there. When Richard and Troy arrived, Troy went straight into the ocean and we took turns with my boogie board. Sometimes we even both got on it. The sun was hot and the water was cold—a perfect California day.

At one o'clock, they called us in for some lunch. Troy and I shared a large towel. We ate a lot because we were starved. We faced the water to tan for a little while. We were close enough to talk without everyone hearing us—even though they probably weren't interested.

I asked, "Does your mom know?"

Troy replied, "Know what?"

"Does she know what your stepdad does to you?"

"I think so. But nobody talks about it."

Richard looked over and asked, "What are you guys talking about?"

I replied, "Nothing."

We stopped talking and looked out at the beach. Troy closed his eyes and I looked at his messy long hair. My hair probably was too. I thought about how little we knew about each other and the secrets we had to keep from the world. We knew the dark side of our lives before we could know the normal side.

I knew Troy was confused by my relationship with Brian. He wasn't my dad or relative and yet I spent all my time with him. Heck, he wasn't even my teacher anymore. But I loved Brian and I needed him. He was the only adult that really took an interest in me. He was a place to escape the madness of my house. Troy would understand soon enough. Over the next week, Brian and Richard made sure we had time together. We liked a lot of the same things and he was easy to hang out with.

Dad was out of town and due back on Friday night. Mom was even worse than usual on Friday. She gave us our list of chores. Before we even started, she was in a bad mood. I knew it would be extra hard to please her. I had to sweep the sidewalks after my brother mowed and clean the bathroom. While Tom mowed, I headed to the bathroom to get started. She reached out and slapped me. I guess she was busy because she kept walking. I made sure I cleaned every inch of the toilet because I didn't want my head in it again. I made sure the sink was extra clean because I wanted to keep my teeth in my mouth.

Sure enough, Mom came in. Before she can even check the bathroom, she said, "Do you think this is clean?" I nodded. This is not the way I had hoped it would go. She grabbed my hair and dragged me to my room. I dug in my heels to slow her down. She was screaming, "This is the thanks I get. All I do for you."

On and on she went. She got to my room and stood me up in front of her and punched me in the face so much I lost count. No matter how I blocked, she hit some part of my head. Her rage finally subsided a little and she quit hitting me. I fell down and rolled to a corner in the room.

"Now go sweep off the sidewalks."

I ran to do it—anything not to get hit again. In the meantime, Dad called and said he couldn't come home that weekend because they hadn't finished the job. When I came back in the house, she went ballistic. My brother and I knew we were dead.

Sometimes Mom would make us go to the yard and cut our own switch. We hoped she liked the one we picked because, if she had to go outside, there was even more hell to pay. She sent us both outside. We worked hard to find just the right size. Not too big, not too small. Neither one of us wanted to walk back in the house. Tom thought if we stayed out a little while she might cool down, but she came looking for us. She was even madder than before. She looked at Tom's switch. She didn't like it. Mine wasn't good enough either. She put them both together and said, "This will work." We would have ran, but past experience had made us smarter than that.

Tom was first; I counted how many hits so I would know what to expect. He was screaming and crying. He was squirming different direction so the switch didn't hit twice in one place. Mom worked his back and legs over real good. I was scared and crying by the time she came to my room. I had no chance to roll in a ball. She was whipping hard. I was squirming and trying to move around. I thought she would never stop. I couldn't even count because the pain was so bad. She left us to our crying. She went to take a nap. I guess all that anger and hitting had made her tired.

The pain was unreal. I had to cry into my pillow. I didn't want her coming in and saying, "Do you want me to give you something to cry about?" I hated that one the most. It sounded like we were overreacting.

Mom woke up and started dinner. Tom and I had both fallen asleep to escape our reality. She acted like nothing was wrong. She called us for dinner and we played along. She made meatloaf, which we both hated. She made peas for Tom because he hated that. She made broccoli for me for the same reason. We had the only mother who enjoyed making food we didn't like in hopes we couldn't eat it. We did well that night. We ate every bite, knowing she just wanted an excuse to punish us again with the switch. It was hard, but it was worth it. I think we felt like we had won a small battle.

It was my turn to do dishes. I knew she would look for any mistake so I did an extra good job washing and drying. I opened a cupboard and two glasses came crashing down and broke on the floor. That's what Mom was waiting for. She came over and punched me so fast I couldn't believe it. I was still standing so she hit and slapped until I fell down on the floor. Then she dragged me to my room for another beating. I was still torn up from the last one. I had no problem begging and pleading for my life. I looked up and she grabbed the switches again. I couldn't believe my bad luck. I counted ten hits before my mind just lost it. She was moving from my back to my butt and then my legs. Next thing I know, she just stopped and walked out of the room. I never knew what made her stop. I crawled under my bed, praying she wouldn't come back—and hoping she would just die.

I stayed there until I knew everyone was asleep. I was in so much pain that I couldn't sleep. I remembered how good Brian made me feel after the last time. In my heart, I knew I had to see him—at any cost. I snuck out ever so quietly. It was scary walking the streets that late at night, but I had done it before and knew I could do it again. I cut through the school and my imagination was running wild. I tried to run, but the pain stopped me right away. I walked as fast as I could and prayed that Brian would be home. I also prayed that God would keep me safe. I prayed my mom wouldn't find out. Finally, I got to his house and saw Roger's car and a few others I didn't know.

I rang the doorbell and Carlos answered. He took one look at me and ran to get Brian. I walked in as Brian and Roger rushed toward me.

Brian said, "Shit, Timmy." He started to carry me, but even that hurt. So he just led me to the bedroom. With gentleness and great compassion and love, he undressed me and then laid me on my stomach on his bed. I was cold and shaking uncontrollably. He put some medicine on my skin. I was crying softly because even that hurt. He gave me a kiss on the forehead and a pill to take for the pain. He stepped out to talk to the others. Carlos came in to comfort me and I fell asleep.

I woke up the next morning in Brian's bed. Troy was sleeping on the floor on my side. I thought to myself, these are the people who really love me. I watched Troy sleep, too afraid to move.

Troy woke up and whispered, "How do you feel?"

Brian said, "You don't have to whisper. I'm awake. How do you feel, Timmy?"

"I hurt."

"I know. Rick brought over some medicine for you last night. You were asleep so we just put it on you. We'll put some more on after you have a bath. Do you want something for the pain now?"

"Will it make me sleepy?"

"Probably, but take it anyway. We'll let it take effect before you get into the bath."

Troy sat down next to me. I only moved my head—I was too scared to move anything else. Brian went to fix my bath. Troy patted my shoulder and said, "I'm sorry."

"Thanks."

The medicine started working while I was trying to walk to the bathtub. The warm water hurt at first and I was begging to get out. Troy was taking everything in and Brian and I could see it was really hard on him. Brian told him to leave and we would be out soon. He left reluctantly.

The pills took most of the pain away. Brian made me soak for a while. He wouldn't leave the room because he was afraid I would fall asleep. And I did. I woke up on the bed wearing one of Brian's T-shirts that reached almost to the floor. It still hurt, but I felt a lot better. It was almost noon and I knew I had at least the afternoon that I could stay here.

I heard sounds in the living room and stumbled my way down the hallway. Brian and Troy were hanging out.

Brian said, "Back from the dead."

I crawled into his lap like a baby with my head against his chest.

When Roger and Carlos came back with lunch, we ate at the kitchen table.

Roger asked, "So Timmy, what happened to you last night?"

Brian gave him a look of disapproval. He knew I didn't need to relive it in front of everyone. I told them the story and there was a long silence.

Carlos asked, "How is your brother doing?"

"I don't know. Should I try to find out?"

"I don't think so. You're not going anywhere right now. Later we will call your mom and you can ask about spending the night at a friend's house."

After lunch, I went to the bathroom to look at my back. There was a lot of damage.

Troy said, "They were a lot worse last night. I can't imagine getting beat like that." I put the shirt back on and he said, "Does your dad know?"

"No."

Carlos had heard the conversation and said, "Yes, he does. You know Troy really likes you. He begged his dad to stay here last night. He wanted to help take care of you. You should thank him."

I was amazed and thanked Troy. I wasn't used to people caring that much.

Carlos said, "Let's go swimming."

Brian walked in the room. I looked at him not sure if I should or not.

He said, "The water will make you feel better."

We headed off to the pool. They walked slower so I wouldn't feel left out. We were used to swimming with nothing on, but Troy still struggled with it. Eventually we all got in. I was unsure of how it would feel on my skin. I moved around some because it felt pretty good. Brian joined us and sat on the top steps. I moved slowly and sat on the step under him.

He called the other guys over to talk.

He said, "There's ten more days until the next party." There went my hopes of no more parties. I guess it had been too much to hope for. "Troy, this will be your first one. Carlos, you know what to do. What about you, Timmy?"

I didn't want to disappoint him or make him mad so I nodded.

Troy looked at me, wondering what he just got himself into. I wondered if he will think it was as screwed up as I did. I felt like I was just surviving in this craziness and doing what I had to do to survive.

We played until Brian and Carlos got out.

Troy asked, "What about the party?"

I could see that his curiosity had gotten the best of him. I wasn't sure if I could explain it without scaring the hell out of him. Heck, I'd been going for over a year and they still scared me.

I said, "These parties aren't for us, just about us. We get paid when it's over."

"How much?"

"It's different each time, but I've never made less than $500."

"You've got to be kidding. What do I have to do?"

"Whatever they tell you to do. You have to remember it's only a game and we're all just acting. But it's different every time. We don't know until it's time to start and they give us instructions." I was done with this conversation so I started to get out of the pool.

"Tell me more."

"That's enough for now." If I told him everything, he could never handle it.

We got out of the pool. Brian told me to call my mom and ask to spend the night at Danny's. I called and asked and there was a real long silence on her end. I couldn't tell what kind of mood she was in.

Finally she asked, "Do you know where your brother is?"

I said, "No."

There was silence again and I was getting nervous. My body couldn't take another beating. I knew she was going to make me come home. The guys were looking at me and my eyes were starting to water.

Finally she said, "Yes."

I thanked her and hung up. Brian walked over and wiped the tear that had slid down my cheek. "Are you okay?"

"Yeah, I guess. Mom can't find my brother."

"He's just doing what you are—staying away from home. Tomorrow will be your day. What do you want to do?"

"The beach."

"The beach it is then. But you can't take your shirt off."

Carlos was smiling because he knew he would go too. Troy called his dad and got permission also.

Brian had been giving me half doses of Vicodin for pain during the day. At nine o'clock, he handed me a whole one and I told him I didn't think I needed it. It still hurt just like a bad sunburn, but I could move around more without hurting. He told me to take it and added another pill to help me sleep. I didn't even question it. He had always been able to help me heal from a beating. We all sat around watching TV and the medicine didn't take long to kick in.

I woke up in my bedroom with Troy sleeping next to me. I was still groggy from the medicine.

Without moving, he said, "Quit staring at me."

"How could you feel that?"

"I just can."

He didn't understand that he still seemed pure and untouched to me. He wanted to enter our world and I wished I could change his mind. I wished I could go back to the time before I was involved in all this.

"Tell me more about the parties. You never really answered my questions last time."

Maybe the truth would scare him enough not to go through with it. Or if he still chose to go, maybe he'd be better off if he knew what was ahead. There was nothing anyone could say to truly prepare a kid for a party like that. I wanted him to realize that once you're in, you're in. There was no getting out. I told him some of the scenarios that had played out, but he didn't seem shocked by the details. I didn't know if he was good at hiding his feelings or actually interested.

Troy asked, "What happened at the last party?"

"I don't want to talk about it."

"Why?" I stayed silent. He said, "I was there."

"You were not!"

"I was the kid in the upstairs window watching you guys with binoculars. I laid there staring at him, dying of embarrassment. There's nothing as bad as someone seeing you in the worst moment of your life. He could see how this affected me and said, "Don't be mad."

"I'm not."

"Don't be embarrassed. I watched you on that cross and that's the reason I am here."

My mind could not grasp that last statement. How could that night of torture willingly draw him into this dark world? I was too shocked to even say anything. He saw the battle going on in my mind. I had been sucked into this world one small, sick step at a time. He had watched safely from a distance and was choosing to enter a sadistic world where pain and pleasure met.

Troy told me the story from the beginning. Brian had been at his house talking to his dad about the parties. Troy could hear through the vents everything that was said. He couldn't believe what he was hearing. It sounded like a secret group where sexual fantasies came true. His stepdad had already introduced him to sex so it seemed like that could be the next step for him. He approached his stepdad and told him that he had heard everything. He was really mad—until he realized he was interested in experiencing it, not telling on them.

He called Brian and he came right back over to address this new turn of events. Brian couldn't take the chance that this new kid would keep the secret. He talked to Troy and his dad. Troy had no problem looking him in the eye and convincing him he was interested.

He said, "I want to go to a party."

Richard said, "Absolutely not!"

Brian knew that once they had you on film or in photographs, there was no turning back. To Brian this was the answer to the problem.

Brian said, "Why not? We've all got kids there."

Richard said, "You can watch, but that's all." His dad knew what they had planned and didn't want his son to have any part of it. "You can't tell anyone about it!"

Troy said, "I haven't told anyone about us." The men couldn't argue with that. "They put me in an upstairs room and locked the door. I saw everything. I watched you watch me. I couldn't believe the excitement I felt. I wanted to be down there with you."

I had tried the truth. I told him the sick stuff. He couldn't grasp what it was like to be on the receiving end of the punishment. He found excitement in it. How was I ever going to convince him to run fast and run far from all of this? "Do you have to go to the next party?"

"No. I don't have to. But I think they will let me."

I used all the authority in my voice that I could and said, "Don't go. This isn't what you think. I wish I could get you to understand."

His mind was already made up, "I want to be there." I knew I was defeated.

We could hear other people moving around the house so we got up and went into the living room. Carlos had slept on the couch so I got a string and tickled his nose. He woke up and grabbed for me, but remembered to be gentle. It was always fun having him around.

We stopped at Winchell's Donut Shop on the way to the beach. It was a great day to be outside. Once I got used to the water, it felt good. I was careful not to let the waves crash into me too hard. At lunchtime, Roger got us Jack in the Box.

Brian motioned for me to sit next to him. "What do you think about Troy?"

"I like him."

"Better than Carlos"

"No. Carlos is like a big brother and Troy is more my age."

"Do you know why Troy is here?"

"Because he likes me."

Brian nodded and said, "You have to draw him into our world."

"That won't be hard. He's dying to get started. He wants to go to another party. He wants the money. I can't even talk him out of it."

"Why would you do that?"

"Because he would be better off."

"Do you think you would be better off?"

I could see the concern on his face. I knew I couldn't have Brian without the parties so I said, "No, I wouldn't. I need you." This made him feel better.

Brian went on to tell me the next step I needed to take with Troy. He reminded me of the night we had stayed with Roger and Carlos. That was the first time I realized how each event was preplanned. I nodded because I knew which night he was talking about. With all that said, we fell silent and watched the waves crash on the shore. I could relate to the ocean.

There were so many events crashing around in my life that I couldn't control; my mom's rage and violence, Brian's friends that partied together every month, Rick and Todd's sadistic world. The ocean and I had a lot in common—we both knew how to take a beating.

After lunch, we went into the water to bodysurf. That was the best part of this day. When I got tired of swimming, I held on to Brian for support. He enjoyed the attention. The men got tired and went to dry off. I tired more easily than usual and went with them. Without thinking, I started to take my shirt off and Brian caught my eye and shook his head. Carlos had come in from swimming. He came up with the idea that I could stay on my back and get some sun on my chest.

We packed up to go home and I sat in the car thinking what a great day it had been. I was nervous because I knew I would have to go home tonight. The best I could hope for was that Dad would be home or Mom would be in a good mood.

After we unpacked the car, I was getting ready to tell everyone good-bye. I heard Brian tell Troy to go take a shower. I was dumbfounded. I wasn't ready for this. I didn't think I would ever be ready or comfortable with this stuff. When I didn't move, Brian said, "Go on, Timmy, you know what to do."

"No, Brian. Please—I really don't want to do this."

"You have to do this." I felt defeated once again.

Troy looked surprised when I walked in, but then he got a big smile. I felt like running back out the door but knew I couldn't. Troy was more than willing to take the next step into our deranged world. It was very hard for me to be the aggressive one.

When we got ready to go to the living room, Troy asked me, "Do you think they know?"

I nodded and hid a smile. He had no idea how they orchestrated our lives. In the living room, the guys looked like their favorite team had won the championship. I was so embarrassed that I wanted to run out of the house.

On the way home, I had time to reflect on everything and wondered why they couldn't just be satisfied with good grades and playing sports and going to the beach. Why did they have to bring sex into everything? I didn't think I would ever know that answer.

A couple of blocks from the house, I ran into the same boys I had successfully avoided for months. They were mad that I had outsmarted them. They were all in high school and I was just going into the fourth grade. What chance did I have?

Josh, the leader, said, "We've got you now!"

I was ready to run, but one of the kids put his arm around my neck and shoulders. Josh looked down at me and said, "Do you have any last words?"

Yep, I'm dead.

He punched me in the gut and I fell to the ground. Josh grabbed my shirt and swung me around so hard that my shirt tore all the way down. I fell and rolled away, pleading for him to stop.

One of the other kids came over and stood me up. He put my hands behind my back so Josh could punch me again. Trying to make a smaller target, I fell to my knees before Josh could get to me. I bowed my head and closed my eyes so I didn't see it coming.

Josh reached out and touched my shoulder and I flinched. He told me to stand up, but his voice was gentle. He took my torn shirt and wiped off some of the dirt and grass. I couldn't believe what was happening. I didn't know what kind of game he was playing with me.

He said, "Your name is Timmy, right?" *He knows where I live and will threaten my family.* I nodded.

"I'm sorry. We didn't mean to be assholes. We were just joking around."

I didn't understand this sudden change of heart. I was the kid who never had good luck. He had me walk beside him and asked, "Who beat you?" I shrugged my shoulders like I didn't know. At least it answered why he was acting so differently. We walked to his bike and he told me to get on his handlebars and I did. The other kids followed us.

We rode by the baseball fields and toward the hills. I wasn't scared because I knew they wouldn't hurt me. He told me to get off and we walked a little ways.

He said, "This is our hideout. You can come here anytime you want. But if you show anybody else, then you're dead. Do you understand?" I nodded. We walked behind a hill and there was a big hole in one of them. It was a cave. I couldn't believe how cool it was. They had it fixed up with couches and mattresses.

"This is where we party. We are having a big one tonight."

He turned me around and walked me back to his bike.

"How many people know about this place?"

"Look, I brought you here to give you a place to hide out or runaway to. Anything like that you can come here. You can wait here for me and or my friends and we will help you. People like us have to stick together. And if anyone wants to fight you, tell them they have to fight Josh Tilford first. Remember you don't have to run from me anymore. We are friends now."

I shook his hand and said, "Thanks a lot."

He told me to ride his bike back to my house and leave it on the side. He would pick it up later. I couldn't believe I finally had a turn of good luck. I could only hope this would hold out at home too.

When I got home, my brother was there by himself. He said, "Mom and Dad went out tonight."

"Where have you been?"

"With friends." I figured that was all the information I would get out of him. I told him my good news.

"If you're nice to me, I will put in a good word with Josh for you."

"Josh Tilford?"

I nodded.

"Bullshit! You're not friends with him."

"I am now—and if anyone wants to mess with me, they have to go through Josh first."

"Bullshit."

"Go look in the yard. I have his bike. He didn't want me to walk home."

Tommy went out and checked and agreed it was his bike.

"Mom left us TV dinners. I'll put them in the oven for us. By the way, can you put in a good word for me with Josh? He's been picking on me when he couldn't find you."

I told him I would. It was funny that the only thing we had in common was our mother's beatings and how we kept the family secret.

CHAPTER TWELVE

TROY' FIRST PARTY

Monday was the next chance I had to return to Brian's house. I let myself in and found out Brian was gone. I found a note in the kitchen. He had gone to Big Bear and wasn't sure when he would be back. I went to the gym to work out first and get that out of the way.

I figured it was time for swimming. I did that until I was tired enough to lie out and relax. I was listening to music when I felt a shadow fall over my body. In the past, this was not good news for me. I didn't want to open my eyes.

I shaded my eyes so I could see and my first thought was he was too short for Rick. I realized I was looking at Troy. I asked him how he got there. He had ridden his bike from his house and was hot and sweaty. I asked if he wanted to get in the pool. I knew the answer and jumped in ahead of him.

We had the best day just being kids. No adults were around to make us do anything we didn't want to. We spent most of the time in the pool. At the hottest part of the day, we went inside and played with my toys. We raided the refrigerator and watched TV.

I said, "What do you want to do?"

"Let's go to your house."

I stared at him in disbelief. "What did you say?"

"Let's go to your house."

"Are you crazy?"

"I have to meet the person everyone talks about."

"You really are crazy."

"What's the worst that can happen?"

"To you, nothing. To me, I could get the living shit beat out of me."

"Come on, Timmy. I will be there to protect you. Come on. We don't have to stay long. I just want to see her."

Troy had the gift of persuasion. I should have stayed strong, but I gave in.

He was excited all the way to my house. He knew me well enough to tell my mind was spinning. He kept trying to lighten my mood. It worked a little—until I got to my driveway. I walked cautiously to the door and listened. Troy found that really strange. All was quiet so I gave him the go ahead.

"Timmy is that you?"

"Yes."

"Come here."

She was in the kitchen.

"Mom, this is Troy." She stared at him for a second.

"Mrs. Fielding, it is very nice to meet you." He reached out to shake her hand. She smiled and shook hands with him.

"It's nice to meet you, Troy."

"You have a really nice house." This scored big points. *Boy, was he smooth.*

"Thank you, Troy. Where do you live?"

"I live in Highland."

"You do? Then how do you know my son?"

"My dad runs the track at the school."

Boy, he's quick too.

"Your dad's a runner. That's good."

"Yes, ma'am."

"Would you like to stay for dinner?"

"Yes ma'am. Can I call my mom to get permission?"

She smiled and pointed to the phone. Mom gave me a look of approval.

When Troy got off the phone, we went to my room and busted up laughing. It was not often that I came out on the winning end with Mom.

"You are really amazing. I have never seen a kid work my mom like that before."

"I don't see the problem. She seems really nice to me." We both started laughing. "So this is your room."

"Yep, this is it."

"I've seen prison cells with more personality."

I looked around and agreed and laughed. My walls had no decorations. I didn't keep anything on top of my dresser because it would look messy. I had no awards to show off. The only color in the room was a plain blue bedspread. We had a good time laughing and joking until it was time for dinner.

Since Dad was home for dinner, nothing weird would happen. We walked into the dining room and Troy introduced himself to my dad. Dad had the same look my mom had. They were wondering how I got such a cool friend—and why his hair was so long. At dinner, Troy was the life of the party. He had us all laughing—even Mom. My brother liked him too.

After dinner, it was time for Troy to go. I asked if I could walk him to the track where his ride would pick him up and my parents agreed. We walked back to Brian's house laughing some more. His stepdad was waiting there for us and he was extremely mad. He was yelling even before he got out of the car. I could tell Brian wasn't home so I left as fast as I could. I went straight home—not even afraid of walking through the door. I should have known better than to ever let my guard down.

Mom yelled, "You're next!"

My brother was in the kitchen with his head shaved. He was crying. *Oh shit,* I thought. I ducked under Mom's arms and ran to the bathroom. I locked the door. It finally made sense—this was about Troy.

Mom yelled, "You get your ass out here right now! You're getting your haircut!" I was thinking fast and hard for a good argument. It was at least worth a try. Before I could think of a good one, she came busting through the door, unlocking it with a screwdriver. She dragged me out by my hair and took me to the kitchen. She pushed me in the chair and I started to fight.

Dad yelled, "That's enough. I'll kick the hell out of you if you move." I sat still and he shaved my head. It didn't take long. I was in total shock.

Mom said, "Only girls have long hair."

I was completely defeated and headed for the bathroom to see if it was as bad as I imagined. I looked in the mirror and felt like crying. It didn't really look bad; other kids had the same haircut, especially during summer. But people picked on me because I was small and looked young. This made it even worse. I looked like I was seven years old.

The next day at Brian's house, I walked in the front door and saw Carlos.

"Timmy, you are busted! What happened to you?"

"Why? What did I do?"

Brian reached out and slapped me across the face, almost knocking me down. I was stunned.

"Do you know how dangerous that was? Letting Troy go to your house? Are you two stupid? This isn't some kind of game!" I could never remember him hitting me like that before. He grabbed me and put me over his knee and spanked me four or five times.

My whole world came crushing down. What if Brian hated me? I started crying hysterically because my heart hurt. I was crushed. I could hear his voice but not his words. I ran for the front door, but he got there first. He picked me up and took me to the bedroom.

"Where did you think you were going?"

I was crying so hard I couldn't answer. He laid me on the bed and I figured there was still more punishment coming. I deserved whatever I'd get.

He whispered to calm me down. Eventually I could even feel his soothing heartbeat.

"Timmy, I love you." I took a deep breath and it felt like a burden had been lifted. I could handle him being upset at me, but I couldn't handle it if he didn't love me anymore. "You are the most beautiful kid in the world."

"I'm sorry, Brian. I am so sorry. I'll never do anything like that again."

"I know. I know. It over, okay? Now just relax. Everything's going to be okay."

I fell asleep. When I woke up he asked, "Do you feel better?"

"Yes. Brian, I am so sorry."

"Shh. It's over. What did your mother do to your hair?"

"She punished me for having Troy over. Now I look so ugly. I look like a baby."

He said, "Trust me. You don't look ugly." I recognized his look. "Quite the contrary—you're more beautiful than ever."

When he started kissing me, I knew he wasn't mad anymore.

Afterward, we went out to the pool.

Roger said, "I know what tomorrow is! The big party—Troy's big day"

I nodded.

Carlos said, "Oh, you're still alive."

Brian said, "That's enough. It's over."

Roger said, "I love the new you."

I smiled and jumped in the pool.

Roger said, "He looks even younger. The guys will be all over him at the party."

Carlos got in the pool and pulled me to the deep end. He didn't want me to hear the end of that conversation. He gently dunked me.

I asked, "Are you mad at me?"

"No. I could care less. But why did your mom cut your hair?" I shrugged. He dunked me again. "Answer my question."

I laughed and said, "To get back at me for having Troy over."

"You're kidding! That bitch!" He dunked me again and then let go of me. I swam around him and crawled on his back for a piggyback ride.

"What did you guys do at Big Bear?"

"A little of this, a little of that."

"Come on. Tell me what you did."

"Nothing really! But what about you and Troy?"

"Troy and I just hung out around here swimming and stuff."

"I think you had more fun than I did."

Brian and Roger were arguing.

Brian said, "He's not going!" He stormed into the house.

Roger yelled, "Yes he is—especially after last time."

He followed him into the house.

I said, "What's up, Carlos?"

"It's about you, Timmy. Just stay out here with me. Let the guys talk."

"What about me?"

"The men are going to be all over you. The younger, the better—and you look younger and better than ever. I think you should demand more money now—because they are going to work you harder than ever."

This was a lot to think about since I couldn't change my looks overnight and I couldn't get out of the party.

When I went in for lunch, Roger was the only one in the kitchen. I never knew what to think of him. He usually didn't pay any attention to me when I was at Brian's. He loved Brian and he put up with me.

He said, "I hope you're happy." I had no idea what he was talking about.

Then he stormed out of the kitchen.

I made myself a sandwich and Carlos came in. I offered to make him one and he took me up on it.

He said, "Where is everyone?" I was as confused as ever. "They're probably in Brian's room."

We spent the next couple hours hanging out and staying out of the way of the adults.

The next day was Saturday. Wishing the day was over didn't work so I went to Brian's as I had planned. Brian's car wasn't there, but Roger's car was. The house was quiet so I went to my room until everyone woke up. I heard some noise and went to the kitchen. Roger and Carlos were there. They hadn't heard me so I went to Brian's bedroom to say hello. He wasn't there.

I went back to the kitchen and asked, "Where's Brian?"

They just seemed unsure about how to answer that question.

Roger said, "He had a family emergency and had to go out of town."

"Do you know when he'll be back?"

"In a few days."

"Okay. I'll see you guys later." I started to walk to the door.

Carlos asked, "Where are you going?"

"Home."

"You get back here." I stopped and looked at him. He said, "We have a party to go to."

"I'm not going if Brian isn't going to be there."

Roger said, "Oh yes you are!"

Carlos said, "Why, Timmy?"

"Who will protect me?"

Roger said, "You don't need anyone to protect you."

I said, "Who will look out for me?"

Roger said, "I will."

"But you don't even like me." I turned back to leave, but Roger stood in front of me and shut the door.

"You don't have a choice. You are going to the party."

"Why? Why do I have to go?"

"Because that's what Brian wants."

I sat on the couch and Carlos sat next to me.

I said, "I can't do this without Brian." Tears rolled down my cheek. "Who will look out for me?"

Carlos put his arm around me and said, "I will. Don't worry. I'll be there for you."

I knew there was nothing he could do. As much as Carlos wanted to help, he was just a kid and we had no power or authority at these parties. All we could be was victims. This was a nightmare come true.

Roger came over and said, "I do like you, Timmy. I promised Brian I would look out for you. Come on, let's go eat some breakfast."

It was only a couple of hours before show time and I dreaded every minute of it.

The parties started around one o'clock. We drove to the same house as the last party and all the bad memories came flooding back. I knew there was no adult to take me away if things turned bad. I had the same fear when Rick and Todd demanded I come over.

We pulled through the double gates and the driveway was full of expensive cars. I stepped out of the car and watched the gates close, wishing I could run for freedom before they locked. It felt like a bad omen.

Carlos said, "Don't worry. Everything will be all right."

He took me straight to the game room to take advantage of this time without the men. Nick and Troy were already playing games.

I walked over to Nick and asked, "Where have you been?"

"Family vacation."

I started playing pinball and listened to the other kids cutting up. For a few minutes, the world felt normal.

A younger guy I didn't recognize came in. He was about twenty with stringy brown hair and looked way too skinny. He walked to where I was playing and leaned against the wall and watched me for a few minutes. I didn't say anything because I was nervous.

"Are you Brian's kid?" I nodded. "How old are you?"

"Ten."

"Which one is Troy?" I pointed to him.

He talked to Troy for a few minutes and left. Roger walked in and told Carlos that it was time to get started. The party was starting out the same as all the others. We undressed in the playroom and raced each other to the pool to start the show.

The pool looked like something from *Blue Lagoon*. There were rock formations and waterfalls and the bottom of the pool had been painted a deep blue. We had fun playing and I was amazed at how relaxed the other boys were. Troy acted like he was an old pro—he had no idea what was ahead.

The men started joining us in the pool. I wondered if any of them were mad at me because of the last party. I could hear the comments and knew they really liked my new haircut. I sensed urgency and hunger in the men. I had never noticed this kind of energy before. They were physically excited a lot earlier than usual.

They knew I liked to do flips and some of the guys took turns. I knew it wasn't for my benefit—it was because they could get some good photographs. After the men got tired, they wanted to play volleyball. We usually played it in the pool. At this house, they had a volleyball court with sand.

I stayed in the water because I liked it better and it brought me some security.

The man from the playroom came to the ledge and said, "Hi, my name is John. Your presence is requested at the volleyball court."

He took me by the hand and led me over there. The men just laughed at me.

Carlos yelled, "Timmy, you're on my team."

I ran to where he was. I was so small I couldn't do the team any good, but everyone around me covered for me. We played until it was time to eat. Nobody really cared who won or lost. That's not what the evening was really about. The real competition hadn't started yet. And the score always stayed the same Men 1, Boys 0.

There was an outside shower so we could rinse the sand off. I was last in line and when I finished, I turned to go inside. John stopped me and rinsed me off for a few more minutes. I didn't like being singled out, but nothing worse happened to me. He just enjoyed touching me.

When I walked in the house, Carlos motioned for me to get in front of him. He helped me make my plate and stayed close to me just as he had promised.

All the kids sat at one table and Carlos gave us his usual pep talk. He reminded us that it was just a game—and everyone was acting. He told me not to freak out. He told Troy to just play along and do as he was told.

Troy said, "What if I don't want to?"

Carlos said, "You don't have a choice now."

I was worried for Troy because this was his first party—and the men had been watching him intently all day.

Roger brought me a cup and a pill. He said, "Take this."

"I don't need it. I'm fine."

"I'm not asking you. I'm telling you." I took the pill and a sip and swallowed. I could taste the wine. "Drink it all." I followed his orders.

After the men ate and drank and conversed, they led us to a huge ballroom. There was plastic on the floor. I remembered doing this before and I hadn't liked it. We were told to put oil on each other. While we did this, the men put on oil too.

Someone brought in two homemade racks. *Oh shit!* They were better made than Rick and Todd's contraptions. It had two beams on the top that held your chest out and two tie-downs for your hands. There was another one that held your stomach up and pushed your butt out with two tie-downs that kept your feet apart. This style gave a lot more access to your body. It was the scariest thing I had ever seen.

If the pills hadn't taken effect, I think my mind would have snapped. I was led to the rack and tied down. My mind was fuzzy; the voices sounded a long way off. Now I was thankful for the drugs Roger had given me.

"You little bastard! You think you can come to my house and ruin my party! Toss me the whip."

The words were getting through the fog in my brain. I could squirm but that was all.

The tie-downs were tight and strong. In the past, the hits mostly just stung and scared me. This guy was mad at me and he started out hitting really hard. His anger was apparent with each swing. It woke me right up and my screams echoed in the room. I guess this wasn't what the men wanted. The next thing I knew, they threw him a ball with a strap on it. He inserted the ball in my mouth and strapped it around my head. This made me crazy. It made it hard to breathe and I was panicking. He took his time working my skin from top to bottom. By then, tears were the only thing left.

I had never been so broken or defeated. I knew this would never have happened if Brian had been there. I couldn't move or scream.

Someone yelled, "That's enough!"

I hung there like I was dead. That wasn't quite the end of my torture. Since he was done hitting me, it was time for what he came for. He walked behind me and raped me.

When the man got off of me, Roger came over and took the ball out of my mouth. I was thankful because I could breathe a lot easier. I wanted to sleep and forget everything, but the pain wouldn't allow it. The rack was not set up for comfort. They brought out a second rack and it was Troy's turn. I wasn't in a position where I could see him. Roger put a pill in my mouth and gave me more wine. I knew this wasn't in the plans; this was Roger having mercy on me. I was thirsty and knew the wine would help the pill work faster so I drank the whole glass of wine quickly. I finally fell asleep with my head hanging down and my body tied to the rack.

I woke up in Carlos's bed wrapped in a sheet. I still had the baby oil on my skin. I hurt from the beating, but not as badly as I had thought I would. My muscles in my legs and butt were the worst and there was pain in my rectum. I stood up slowly, lost my balance, and fell. My head was spinning and I had a headache. I called for Carlos.

"What the hell happened?"

Carlos helped me back into the bed. Roger came back in with another pill and a glass of water. I didn't resist. Troy looked really sad.

I asked, "Are you okay?"

He shrugged and asked, "Do you feel as bad as you look?"

Carlos said, "He'll be all right. We're going to get him cleaned up. He won't feel anything soon enough."

I made it to the tub and they helped me clean up. On the way back to the bed, I knew it was just in time. The last thing I saw before I fell asleep again was Brian's face. I tried with all my strength to open my eyes to see if he was really there with me.

The next time I woke up, I was wearing one of his shirts. I could hear him in the bathroom. He heard me moving and came in to check on me. I was so glad to see him and so pissed at him at the same time.

He asked softly, "Are you okay?"

"You made me go without you! You promised me you would be there! You said you'd never let anyone hurt me! You lied to me! You weren't there for me! You knew what they were going to do to me and that's why you weren't there!"

He let me get it all out. He sat on the bed and held me close.

"I'm so sorry, Timmy. They wouldn't let me come. That was the price I had to pay for helping you last time."

"Then you should have made sure I didn't go either."

"I know. I know."

We sat like that for a while. I wondered how I had gotten from being Brian's special boy to being tied to a rack in front of strangers. If I thought too long or too hard, I would know I should leave Brian—and I couldn't handle that.

"How am I going to explain the marks on my back and legs to my parents?"

"Your mom will think she did it."

I felt like defending her after what he had put me through. "She's not stupid, Brian!"

"You'll see. The marks will heal up without your parents ever seeing them."

I just wished the damage done to my mind would heal. I had nightmares for months after that party. I was more scared of that group and their parties than anything. Sometimes just thinking about them would push me over the edge—and I would break down and cry.

CHAPTER THIRTEEN

REVENGE

For the next couple of weeks, Brian really spoiled me. He really wanted to make it up to me. I enjoyed the extra attention. We went to the beach as often as we could. We worked out every day. Some days, Carlos and Troy or even Nick came over. I was developing more of my own personality. I felt more confident about making decisions for myself. I knew there was a big party coming up and I had something to tell Brian.

Roger and Brian were talking at the kitchen table. For two weeks, I had been practicing. I walked over to Brian and put my arms around his shoulder.

I said, "You need to tell the guys something for me."

Brian said, "What guys?"

"The guys who go to the parties."

"Tell them what?"

"If they ever whip me like that again, I'm telling."

Roger yelled, "No one will listen to you!"

"Maybe. But I'm telling just the same."

I was standing between them. Roger grabbed me by the throat and yelled, "Who the hell do you think you are!"

"I'm a scared kid, Roger. I can't sleep at night. And when I do, I have nightmares. I'm scared all the time."

Roger slapped me really hard. I held my face, feeling the burn in my check. I glared at him. I was scared but knew that I couldn't back down. My eyes began to fill up with tears.

Brian stood there in shock.

I turned on my heels to walk away, but Roger grabbed my arm. "Don't you walk away from me." He swung me around. Before I knew what was happening, he threw me against the wall—and I bounced onto the floor. I was crying. I stood up and stared at both of them.

Carlos came to the doorway to watch what was happening. I stood my ground and didn't back down. Brian yelled at Roger to stop it.

Carlos said, "You can tell them if he doesn't, I will. I'm sick of it! You hate his mom for beating him and then you let your friends do the same thing to him. How screwed up is that!" He walked over to me and took my arm to lead me out. "You guys think about that. We're going swimming."

Carlos took me outside and we looked at each other in total disbelief of how brave we had just become. I said, "Thanks. You're a good friend."

Brian came out and said, "Carlos, did you put him up to this?"

Carlos shrugged . "It's something we talked about."

I said, "Brian, are you mad at me?"

"Yes. You should have talked to me alone first." I had no idea how right he was about that. "What's wrong with your arm?"

The pain was really kicking in. Brian asked to see my arm. I showed it to him.

"Shit, Timmy. It's broken!"

Brian walked me back into the house. He yelled, "You son of a bitch. You broke his arm."

Roger said, "I know. I heard it snap. Timmy, please forgive me. I'm so sorry. I am so ashamed of myself."

I was crying because of the pain. Brian said, "Look, Timmy, you just fell off your bike—that's how you broke your arm. Okay?" I nodded. "Timmy, you were never here today. Go home and show your mom your arm."

Brian wasn't even going to give me a ride home.

Roger said, "I swear to God, Timmy, I'll never touch you in anger again and I won't let anyone else either."

I nodded.

Carlos walked me out to my bike. He said, "Remember, Timmy. You fell off your bike."

It was so hard riding my bike across the field with one arm. I couldn't do it anymore. I got off my bike and started crying my eyes out, not just about my arm, but what just happened between Roger and

I. A boy and his dad were playing catch. They noticed me and the boy asked me what was wrong. I showed him my arm.

He yelled, "Dad, he's hurt."

His dad came across the field and looked me over. He asked me where I lived. I told him where I lived and he picked me up and told his son to bring my bike. He carried me all the way home, knocked on my front door and told my mom where he had found me.

Mom thanked him and called my dad. He met us at the hospital. We sat in the emergency room for what seemed like forever. I realized that it was Rick and Todd's hospital. For the first time, I wished they were there.

When my name was called, the doctor put a cast put on my arm. He also gave me a shot for the pain and a prescription. I was so glad it had stopped hurting. I was scared when it was time to leave because I didn't know if I was in trouble for putting my parents out. They weren't mad though and they took me out for ice cream before taking me home.

The next week, I didn't feel well and Mom made me stay home. She was nice and sympathetic. She was really depressed and when she wasn't drinking, she was popping pills and sleeping. I knew she was a time bomb waiting to go off—and I didn't want to be there when that happened.

It had been a week since I'd seen Brian or anyone in the group. He called a few times and I kept him up on my progress. I had been asking Mom almost every day if I could go out. To my surprise, she finally said yes. I left the house as fast as I could to see Brian.

It was after eight o'clock when I got there. Roger's car was there so it probably meant Carlos was too. Not wanting to wake them up, I checked for my key. I unlocked the door and Carlos was sleeping in my bed. I curled up next to him. He opened his eyes enough to see that it was me.

"Timmy, I sure have missed you."

He wrapped his body around me and we fell asleep.

An hour or so later, I could feel Carlos watching me.

"Stop staring at me."

"Oh my God, Timmy! How can you tell?"

I guess I sensed it. When I opened my eyes, Carlos had his arm bent holding up his head. He looked so relaxed, staring at me.

"Carlos, what are you thinking about?"

"Just you."

"What about me?"

"Timmy, you caused a lot of problems with that fight you and Roger had. Roger is sorry as hell at how he hurt you. But some of the guys are madder than hell at how you threatened the whole group. You threatened to expose them."

"Yeah. But you backed my play."

"No, Timmy. I told them the truth. Timmy, they live their lives for this secret. They would rather die than be exposed."

"Don't you mean they would rather kill me than let me expose them?"

"This is no fucking joke, Timmy."

"You know I would never really tell, right?"

"It doesn't matter what I think."

"Please, Carlos. I don't want to die. I'm just tired of being scared and beat all the time."

"I know, Timmy, but it's not me you have to convince."

"You won't let them kill me, right?"

"Of course not, Timmy—but I'm just a kid like you."

"What should I do?"

"Suck up to the right people, starting with Roger. You already have Brian, but suck up to him too."

I rolled off the bed, protecting my cast.

Carlos said, "Where are you going?"

"To suck up!"

I ran straight into Brian's room. Roger and Brian were awake. I jumped on the bed, surprising them. Brian spun me around really fast, pinning me down.

"My arm! My arm!"

Brian jumped off me really quick. "Oh my God, Timmy."

I looked at him and laughed as I said, "Sike."

Brian thought that was really funny, but Roger didn't know what to think. I rolled over to Roger so we were touching. I put my hands behind my head as I stared up at the ceiling. They were staring at me.

I said, "Roger, I'm sorry."

"For what?"

"I didn't mean to piss you off the other day."

"Yeah right! I break your arm—and you're sorry? Who have you been talking to?"

"Carlos. But I came here this morning on my own, and I'm telling you on my own without Carlos being here. I am sorry and I want things back the way they were before." I was also thinking that I don't want to die. I already know what these guys are capable of. I also know I don't want my friends or family to know what I've been doing. I also know I love Brian and need him. I don't want to lose Carlos or Troy. I could do without Roger and the rest of the group, but they're a package deal.

After a long silence, Roger said, "I'll forgive you if you forgive me."

"Done," I said.

CHAPTER FOURTEEN

A NEW YEAR

The new school year started and I was in the fourth grade. I was nervous because I wouldn't have Brian to make me feel special. The teacher's name was Ms. Noel and it was her first year. She was young and pretty.

The first day felt like a reunion. It was comforting to know I was still popular. From my desk, I could look out the window and see Brian sometimes. That was cool. I was putting my stuff away when I heard my name over the intercom system. I was told to go to his classroom. I took off at a run and walked in the door smiling. I knew I was allowed to so I went and gave him a hug too. He introduced me to the class and announced that I would be his student helper. He looked at me and explained that it had already been cleared with Ms. Noel. This would make the school year even better.

While the kids were busy, I told Brian that I could see him when he stood in a certain spot. To my surprise, he announced to all the kids that they were moving the room around. They had no idea why and didn't really care. When it was done, I had a clear view of Brian anytime I wanted to look across the hall. Things like that always let me know how special I was to him.

After school, I hurried to Brian's house and ended up beating him home. I was waiting on the couch when I heard his car pull in. I ran outside and attacked him. I was so happy at how everything was turning out. He picked me up and threw me over his shoulders and laughed. He put me on the floor and we wrestled for a minute. He asked if I had homework and I told him no.

After we worked out, I said, "I have to go home."

"Why?"

"Mom told me to come home right after school."

"Well you blew that, didn't you?"

I went to the front door of my house and listened—everything was quiet. I walked in and heard a crash and immediately felt pain. Mom was hiding behind the door and had hit me in the back of the head with a pan. It wasn't the first time she had done that. Each time a pan hits you in the head, it has its own distinct sound. I fell to the floor. She swung it like a bat. Her aim was good because she never missed hitting some part of me. I was balled up and rolling away each time she swung. She beat me until it got too heavy.

I ran to my room. My brother came in and he had gotten the hell beaten out of him too.

"Were you late too?"

He shook his head. "No. You would have gotten it no matter what time you got home."

After school on Thursday, I started for Brian's house. Nick was at the playground and yelled, "Timmy, come here."

"What are you doing here?"

"Rick is here to pick you up."

"Why?"

"To finish the movie."

"We already did that."

"We're starting a new one."

"Please, Nick, just tell them you couldn't find me."

"No. Come on. Let's just get it over with."

He walked me to the side exit where Rick was waiting.

At their house, everything seemed normal. Nick went to the refrigerator and got us Cokes.

Rick said, "It's going to be about thirty minutes."

I asked, "Can I go swimming?"

He nodded. I ask Nick to come along, but Rick said no. This was odd, but I went outside by myself. I swam for a while and then sat in the Jacuzzi until Rick called me.

The garage had the rack from the party in there and more toys and accessories than ever.

Todd said, "Do you like?" He was enjoying how nervous all this made me. "Just stop. You know Rick and I aren't going to hurt you. " I knew better than to believe an adult when they said that. He finishes, "Just get on the rack. You know how it works."

I did as he said—as if I really had a choice. He got the straps tightened and all I could move was my head.

He whispered, "But there's someone here that is dying to hurt you."

I was hoping that was only a line in the movie, but Rick walked out and a guy with a mask walked in. I figured it was Todd. The build was similar. Without saying anything, he walked over to the table and grabbed the whip.

He turned to me and said, "You little piece of shit!" I knew that voice and I knew I was in for it. "You threaten me!" Whip. "You're going to tell on me!" Whip.

Roger took off his mask. *Yep, I'm dead.* I started to yell for help, but I realized that no one would come. He put the ball in my mouth.

Now I can't even plead with him. "Timmy, Timmy, Timmy." He pulled my head up by my hair to look me in the eye. "I've watched most of your little home movies here. I wonder if your parents will find them as entertaining as I have—or maybe your classmates. Wouldn't that make a hell of a show-and-tell at school?" I dropped my head. "I see your mother has already gotten to you. Good. She won't be able to tell what's new. Now, let's take our time and make sure you learn your lesson well."

Nick walked in and said, "Can I watch?"

Roger nodded and went to work on my back, butt, and inner thighs. I was squirming and crying. I looked over at Nick and all I saw was his approval. He was smiling and enjoying it. It hurt—but wasn't as bad as the guy at the last party. Roger stopped and handed the whip to Nick.

Nick said, "You tell on them, you tell on all of us. This stays private. Do you get it?"

He whipped me ten times—and some hit between my legs. I was dying of pain. It felt like someone had kicked me in the balls, but worse. They laughed and walked out.

After a couple of minutes, Nick came back and took the ball out of my mouth, but he left me tied. I thought, so much for being brave and standing up to everyone. A kid just can't win in this world. Brian can only protect me so much. When I'm not with him everyone else can still get me. I don't know if I will ever be able to make my own choices in life.

When Nick came in to untie me, he said, "Stop crying, you little pussy."

He grabbed my arm and pushed me outside toward the pool. All the guys were sitting in the Jacuzzi. Nick was still the brave bully and pushed me in the pool. Rick motioned for me to join them in the Jacuzzi and I swam over.

I got in slowly, knowing that it hurts at first and then feels better. The men stared at me and it was really intimidating because I knew I had threatened their secret group. I saw a new kind of mad on their faces.

Todd said, "It's over. Did you learn your lesson?"

I didn't trust my voice so I nodded.

Todd said, "Are you going to tell?"

I shook my head.

He whispered, "No more crying."

I nodded again.

"Don't even think about telling Brian or Carlos."

I nodded again.

Nick asked, "Are you mad at me." I nodded. "You big baby. You know it didn't really hurt."

I said, "Then let me do it to you."

"Why? Don't you think I can take it?"

"No. I don't think you could."

"Okay, you can do it to me. I'll prove to you what a wimp you really are." He got in the pool and swam to the edge.

I didn't think he was serious, but I played along.

We walked to the garage and he said, "Go ahead. Tie me down."

I did it as fast as I could before he changed his mind. I picked up the whip and said, "Now you're mine."

I picked up the ball and walked in front of him.

He said, "You won't need that."

"Bullshit."

I put the ball in his mouth. I gave his butt five good swings. His face turned red. I could see tears forming in his eyes. I let him know I was only warming up. After five more on his back, he was squirming. I started working his butt and thighs over really good like he was trying to get loose. Now he was really crying. I hit him five more times really hard between the legs.

I took my victory walk to the front of the rack and said, "Why are you crying? It doesn't really hurt."

I took the ball out of his mouth and he was gasping to catch his breath.

Nick said, "I'm going to kill you!"

I put the ball back in his mouth.

"I didn't give you half of what I got. Do you want the other half?"

His eyes lit up and he shook his head. He bowed his head in defeat. I knew he had experienced some of what I had been through. I took the ball out of his mouth, untied him quickly, and ran back to the pool.

I went out to the Jacuzzi and sat down.

Rick said, "No. He didn't actually let you?"

I nodded and the men started laughing.

Nick walked outside and said, "Get over here, you little bastard!"

I smiled smugly. "Why?"

"I'm going to kick your ass."

Roger said, "Nick, get over here."

Nick didn't move, trying to look tough.

"Get over here right now!"

Nick sat down next to Roger.

"What's your problem?" Roger asked.

Nick stood up and turned around to show them the marks. I was proud I had gotten him pretty good.

Roger said, "You call Timmy a baby—look at you."

Nick was wiping tears from his eyes. He said, "You didn't hit him half as hard as I got it."

I said, "Bullshit!" I stood up and showed them my marks. "What are you complaining about? You asked me to do it. I still only gave you half of what I got."

He ended the conversation by getting in the swimming pool. The guys were laughing at him for making such a stupid decision. He gave up being mad at me and we spent the rest of the time hanging out together.

CHAPTER FIFTEEN

MOVING

A couple of weeks later, I was told to stay home on Saturday. The whole family had special cleaning chores. Dad was home so Mom probably wouldn't get out of hand. Tom and I thought it was strange to do so much cleaning with no one coming over. We had cleaned all day and Dad had made an appointment for a real estate agent to come out.

I asked Tom, "Did you know Mom and Dad were putting the house up for sale?"

He shook his head.

While they were filling out the papers and talking prices, there was a knock at the door. He was an Asian man and I couldn't understand his question. I called Dad over to help me.

He asked, "How much for the house?"

Dad told him the asking price and he said, "I buy your house."

I couldn't believe what I was hearing. I felt like the whole world had gone mad. Mom called us into the living room and told us we would be moving in two months.

I said, "Where are we moving to?"

"To Yorba Linda—it's about a half hour from here. We're getting a bigger house in a better neighborhood. Even the schools are better."

And that was that. Out of nowhere we were moving.

I couldn't believe my bad luck. I finally liked school. I had friends and a life with Brian. That night, I cried myself to sleep. The next morning was Sunday and we drove to Yorba Linda and went house-hunting instead of going to church. We looked at ten or twelve houses until my parents found the one they wanted. This one made our old house look like a dump. The price was right and they started doing the paperwork right away. One part of me knew it was a step up. I liked the house a lot better and my room was great, but how did all that compare to what I would have to give up?

On Monday morning, I left as soon as my dad walked out the door. It was about 5:30 and I knew I had to break the news to Brian. It was going to be the hardest thing I had ever had to do. I didn't want to talk to him at school. I wanted the security of his house. I went to his room and took off my shirt and shoes.

He said, "Oh God, Timmy. It's too early."

"I know. I just couldn't sleep."

I crawled right into his chest. He wrapped himself around me and for a while the world was right. I still couldn't sleep, wondering what life would be like without Brian.

He said, "Are you okay?"

"Yes."

I couldn't imagine where I would be if it weren't for him. I fantasized that he would take me and run away to Big Bear—and it would just be the two of us. No one would ever find us.

His alarm went off and he said, "Don't get me wrong, Timmy. I love when you wake me up in the mornings, but—" He rolled over and started to tickle me.

"Brian, I have something to tell you." He thought I was playing. I had used that line in the past. "No, really."

He stopped and sat next to me. "Okay, what?"

"We're moving."

"What do you mean you're moving?"

"We have to move to Yorba Linda."

"Bullshit."

"No, really"

"Timmy, you better not be screwing around. Are you?"

"No, I'm not."

"Have your parents put your house up for sale yet?"

"Yes."

"That piece of shit won't sell."

"It already did."

He told me to get dressed because he wanted to see the sold sign himself. We got in the car and drove in silence.

When he saw the sold sign, he said, "Oh shit, Timmy." He couldn't believe it. He turned around and headed back to his house. "How long?"

"Two months."

He had tears in his eyes. We walked back inside. I was mentally willing him to say the things I wanted to hear. *Come live with me. We will run away and no one will find us. I wish you were my son. I won't let them do this to us.* But he didn't. He got ready to go to school.

It was hard to concentrate. I daydreamed for most of the day until it was time to help in Brian's room. It was the last hour of the day. His kids were working on a book report. He stared into space, his mind a hundred miles away. I sat quietly, glad to be close to him. Then it hit me and I looked around the room.

Who would be Brian's new boy? He paid a lot of attention to that kid named Brett. I was getting mad. I didn't want to be replaced. I didn't want another kid in my room playing with my stuff. I didn't want to move! The bell rang and I ran out of the class. Brian was yelling for me to come back.

I ran as hard and fast as I could. I ran past my house, over the railroad tracks, and into the cave. I never thought I would need Josh's offer because I had a safe place to go. No one was around and it was dark and a little scary. My eyes adjusted and I sat on the couch. I thought the older guys would be coming by after school. It was quiet and eventually fell asleep.

A few hours later, a crashing noise woke me up. It sounded really close and I realized it was a train whistle. I knew it was time to go home.

I listened at the door and it sounded like they were in a good mood. Mom was really excited about moving. As long as she was happy, we were safe. I got ready for dinner and the phone rang.

Tom answered it and said, "It's for you."

Brian said, "Are you all right?"

"Yes."

"I know this isn't your fault. Come over early tomorrow."

We said good-bye and hung up.

Dad asked, "Who was that?"

"Danny."

End of discussion. Dinner tasted good and everyone was happy. I acted happy for their sake.

On the way to Brian's house, I was really sad. I knew that nothing would be the same again. Who could love me like Brian did? I went to the bedroom and crawled in next to him.

He held me and said, "I'm sorry, Timmy. I love you. I'm just hurting right now. I don't want to lose you."

I knew this was my chance to speak up. I said, "You don't have to. Let's run away together."

I wanted him to be excited about my idea. I wanted him to jump up and start packing and say we could leave now. He held me and I started crying softly.

He whispered, "Timmy, it will be all right."

I fell asleep dreaming of Big Bear.

When I woke up, Brian was already in the kitchen cooking breakfast. I looked at the clock and saw it was nine o'clock. We were late for school, but he told me he had already taken care of it. We were going to spend the day together.

"The weather is good. We could go to the beach. It's been a long time since we've been to the beach alone."

I smiled back at him.

We went to the bedroom after breakfast and he got the water ready for a shower. He undressed me and I acted shy. Even though I was past that, he still liked me to act. He was extra gentle and tender in a way I hadn't seen him in a long time. He was taking in every minute with me like he was memorizing it.

We left for the beach and Brian said, "Timmy, don't tell anyone you're moving."

"Why?"

"Trust me—we don't want them knowing."

"Won't we still be able to see each other? It's only Yorba Linda? You could pick me up."

"I don't know yet. But you have to listen to me. I'm very serious. You can't say anything to Carlos or Troy or any of them. Do you understand? This isn't a joke. They can't know. It should be easy for you; after all, you are the Fort Knox of secrets."

Oh shit. I had only used those words with Rick and Todd. But he didn't say any more on that subject. I never would know what the men had told each other.

I knew what Brian was telling me. I already knew to be afraid of all the men in the group. They had made sure of that from the first time I met them. I knew all the blackmail they had on me. I hadn't told yet, but I was still under their control. I knew they would feel like I was a loose end that needed to be taken care of. Brian could only protect me so much and then it was out of his control. The smartest thing I could do was slip away quietly and unexpectedly and let Brian convince the men I wouldn't talk. I wanted to know if any part of my future included Brian, but this was not an answer he was ready to give me yet. That made me nervous.

We put our stuff on the beach and headed right out to the water. We bodysurfed for a while and then Brian carried me into deeper water. It was great holding onto him and knowing I was safe. If only that day would never end. We walked the pier and he bought ice cream. We sat on a bench and watched the waves.

On the way home, I said, "I don't want to leave."

"I know, Timmy. I know."

We were both silent after that. I was thinking of our good times together. We pulled into the driveway and Brian told me it was late and I needed to go home.

Things were great at home. Mom and Dad were excited about the move. Mom had always thought our house was beneath her—and she deserved much better. In her mind, this new house would fix everything. Other people's perceptions meant everything to Mom and she was moving up.

The kids at school had seen the sold sign so there was no keeping a secret with them. Brian was nervous because so many people were finding out so fast. The kids seemed sad that I was moving. It made me feel good that I would be missed, but I was sad about losing my friends. It told me that I wasn't just popular when Brian was the teacher. I had done some of this on my own.

Danny walked in with tears in his eyes. I told him that we would still be friends and I wasn't moving too far away. I told him I would still be able to see him. I was beginning to understand how hard these next two months were going to be.

After school, I went to Brian's house.

"Timmy, this is going to be harder than I thought to keep quiet—especially with a sold sign in your yard!

"Brian, it's okay. Nobody from the group knows where I live."

"Oh really, Timmy? No one! What about Troy—or Carlos, Roger, Rick, and Todd? And God knows who else?"

I wondered how he knew that Rick and Todd knew my address. It made me wonder if Brian was the one who told them. How much else did he know about Rick and Todd? I was too afraid to ask.

"If anyone asks, we will tell them you're not moving very far away. Get in the car and we will find a house with a sold sign around here and tell them that's where you're moving."

We drove around and found one that fit our story. Brian felt better having a game plan.

At Roger's house, Brian paused in the driveway and reminded me to keep our stories straight. I nodded. Roger opened the door, looked at me without smiling, and pointed for me to go straight to Carlos's room. I ran up the stairs, but before I got to his door, I silently snuck up on Carlos. He was writing at his desk. I put my hands over his eyes. I didn't speak because he would know my voice.

"Aren't you supposed to say guess who?" I nodded his head yes for the answer, still silent. "Then say it. I know it's you, Timmy."

Then he pulls my hands to his chest and I put my head on his shoulders and ask, "What are you doing?"

"Homework, but I am tired of it. I need a break. The pool is warm. Do you want to go swimming?"

I quickly answered, "Yes."

We raced down the stairs, undressing as we went. We slid into the kitchen at the same time. Brian saw where we were headed and opened the glass door that led to the pool. He stepped in front of Carlos to give me the lead and I jumped on this opportunity.

I jumped in the pool first and Carlos was yelling that I was a cheater. We both started laughing. It dawned on me that there was no way my parents would let me run through the house—especially if I was half-naked. That thought made me laugh even harder. Carlos thought I was mocking him so he swam under the water and pulled me down.

We got to the top at the same time. Carlos was laughing and I was trying to catch my breath. Brian and Roger had walked to the side of the pool.

Roger said, "Stop for just a minute. We are going out for a couple of hours. Do you think you two can behave yourself until then?"

I nodded, but Carlos laughed and said, "No."

Roger said, "Don't eat anything. We will bring dinner back with us."

As they walked away, I swam to the shallow end. The air was cold so I walked to where only my head was out of the water.

Carlos swam up to me, then circled me and finally stood in front of me.

"Do you have something that you want to tell me?" I looked him in the eyes. "Do you have something you want to tell me?" He was backing me to the side of the pool. His mood had changed at that point and he was not laughing. "I'm not screwing around, Timmy! Do you have something you want to tell me?"

I was getting nervous and I said, "I don't think so."

He reached out and dunked me.

"What about now? No secrets, Timmy!"

I had no idea what he was talking about. I didn't think he could know about my house selling already—or could he? He dunked me again and I pushed off the side and swam away.

I needed some space to think. I didn't even know what he was talking about. I'd seen Carlos mad, but hardly ever at me. He grabbed my arm and punched me in the face. He busted open my top lip and gave me a bloody nose. I start to cry because I didn't know why this is happening.

"Do you have something you want to tell me?"

"Please, Carlos, stop."

He dunked me and held me under the water. I see the blood from my nose and lip. I was under long enough that I started to panic. He let me up, but kept me in his grip.

"Do you have something you want to tell me?"

I nodded. I was totally defeated. He walked me over to the steps and told me to sit down.

"My mom and dad put our house up for sale and I'm moving away."

Carlos's mouth dropped open. Obviously, that wasn't the news he was waiting to hear. I was sitting there like a whipped puppy. I was scared and cold and my face was bleeding.

"Do you have anything else you want to tell me?"

When I shook my head, he grabbed my arms and started dragging me into the deep end. I freaked out and tried to get away. He turned around and jumped on my head and held me under. I didn't have time to hold my breath so I sucked in water as I went under.

When he let me up, I was choking and spitting water. Carlos grabbed me by the neck and I threw up. He let go and jumped back and got out of the pool quickly.

"Shit, Timmy, Roger is going to kill you."

I turned back to the shallow end and sat on the steps. I was wasted mentally and physically exhausted. Carlos acted like the pool was condemned and sat on the ledge.

"Our lives are full of secrets and you expect me to know which one you're talking about?"

I started looking for my clothes. I put them on as I found them. After I was dressed, I walked out the front door and sat on the steps. I put my head on my knees and tried to figure out what had happened. Carlos—my mentor, my protector, and my friend—had turned on me like a wild animal.

Carlos walked out and put his arm around me. I was shaking because I was still wet and cold.

Carlos said, "I'm sorry." I watched my tears hit the ground. "Come inside. You're freezing." I didn't move. "Timmy, please come inside. I'm really sorry."

I just looked at him. He finally saw how devastated I was. He tightened his arm around me and kissed my cheek. "Timmy, please, I'm sorry. We need to talk before the guys get home." He grabbed me by my arms, pulled me up, and led me back in the house.

Carlos said, "Let's go to my room." I stopped and he saw the fear in my eyes. He said, "Timmy, I said I was sorry. I'm not going to hurt you." He took me to the bathroom and handed me a towel. I looked in the mirror at my fat lip. He helped me wipe my face and fixed my hair. We go to his room and I sat on the bed while Carlos took a chair and faced me. "Are you all right?"

"You just hit me and almost drowned me and scared the hell out of me! And I still don't know why!"

"Tell me what happened the last time you were at Rick and Todd's house." He could see the surprise on my face. "Yes, Timmy, I know. What I don't know is why you never told me. " I didn't know how much he knew. "Why didn't you tell me? I could have helped you."

"Tell you what, Carlos? You know how they are. You know they scare the hell out of me. You—of all people—know what they are capable of. How could I tell?"

"All I know is that I stood up for you that day in Brian's house. When Roger and I got home, I had never seen him so furious. I thought he was going to kill me. He beat the hell out of me. I put myself on the line for you and you still kept secrets from me."

"So you're mad at me? What do you think he did to me at Rick and Todd's house? Trust me—there wasn't any mercy shown there! And by the way, Carlos, I didn't ask for your help!'

Carlos grabbed my shirt and screamed, "You little shit! I've been looking out for you since the day I met you!" He sat on my stomach and pinned my arms down. I didn't even resist. "Are you tired of me looking out for you?"

"Carlos, that's not what I'm saying. I'm sorry. I didn't mean it that way. I'm grateful for all you've done. Please don't be mad. I need you."

He rolled over next to me. We were silent for a few moments.

"Carlos, I'm really sorry. Please don't be mad. I need you."

"Okay. Hell, I forgot. What do you mean you're moving away?"

"It's true, I'm moving." I explained how it had sold the first day and how we had found our new house already. I told him about my talk with Brian. I was nervous and talking real fast, not leaving anything out. "But I'm not supposed to tell you, Roger, or anybody. Brian said it's for my own safety."

Carlos's eyes were shiny with tears. He said, "He's right. If the men found out, you wouldn't be safe. You can't tell anyone—especially Roger. Don't even tell Brian what we talked about tonight." I nodded. He reached out and touched my fat lip. "I'm sorry, Timmy."

"What will we tell Brian and Roger?"

"We'll tell them you got a fat lip playing in the pool. Let's go get the pool clean before they come back."

We got the pool cleaned in time and the guys brought back pizza and the rest of the evening went smoothly.

CHAPTER FIFTEEN

A FAVOR FOR TROY

The next couple of weeks were uneventful. On Thursday, I stayed after to help Brian straighten up the classroom. When we were done, I raced him back to the house and won. I never understood how I beat him when he drove home from school. I turned on the TV, sat on the couch, and acted like I had been there for hours.

When Brian walked in, he said, "Well, Speedy Gonzalez, let's see if you're ready to work out." By then I knew his whole routine.

A few minutes into it, Brian said, "You know there's a party on Saturday?" I nodded. I didn't care because I knew it would be my last one. I knew it would be the last time they could hurt me. "Aren't you going to try to talk your way out of it?"

"Why? Do I have a chance?"

He shook his head and did another set. He finished his set before I was done and came over to me. He undid my pants and led me to his room to take a shower.

On Saturday, I got up when it was still dark and used my key to get into Brian's house. He always acted like he didn't want me to come over early, but I know he liked that time. I stood by the bed and took off my shirt and shoes and socks.

"Oh God, Timmy, it's too early for you." He lifted the covers and we both fell asleep for a few hours.

We met Richard and Troy at Denny's for breakfast. I was excited to see Troy because I hadn't seen him since the last party.

Troy was unusually quiet. There was none of his cockiness. I had been afraid this would happen once the guys got hold of him. They totally broke you down and then swore you to secrecy. Silence was the code of ethics they demanded.

"What's wrong, Troy?"

"Nothing."

"What have you been up to?"

"Nothing!"

I went to the bathroom and Troy followed. We got inside and Troy broke down and cried.

"What's wrong?"

"I can't ... I can't ... I can't keep doing this."

"Doing what?" I knew the answer. God only knows what the men had been making him do.

"I don't want to go to the party today. I'm afraid."

My heart was breaking for him. This was why I tried so hard to talk him out of it. I knew for the first time that I had a way out and it was coming soon. Troy had no way out and his stepdad was involved too.

I said, "It's only a game. They won't really hurt you."

"Bullshit, Timmy. You know that isn't true!"

I didn't know what to say. Of course it wasn't true—but if you said the lie often enough, you might believe it.

Troy tried to calm down and wiped his face. "You were right. I should have never gotten involved."

"What's going on, Troy? Why are you so upset?"

"My stepdad has been taking me over to Rick and Todd's house. Now I know that's why they have been leaving me alone. He continues, "I know you know about it, Timmy. I've seen your movie." I didn't know what to say, but I wasn't surprised. I had no idea how many people had seen that movie. "On Monday, they are coming for you." *Like hell they are.*

"Thanks for the warning."

"No, Timmy, please. I need you to be there. I am so scared. I don't want to be alone."

He started crying again. I really felt sorry for him. I knew exactly what he was going through. I put my arm around him and told him it would be okay. He was twelve and I was only ten, but I felt like the older one.

"Promise me you'll be there."

"I promise."

"Please stay with me at the party today. Don't let me out of your sight. I need to know you're there."

"I promise."

He made me swear. We tried to make it look like he hadn't been crying. The guys didn't notice so I guess we did a good job. Troy started to relax a little. God only knew what Rick and Todd have been doing to him. I got cold chills knowing I was going to find out on Monday. I knew I couldn't worry about it now; there was enough going on today to worry about. I put it out of my mind and did my best to keep Troy relaxed.

After breakfast, we went to Roger's house for the party. We helped get the house ready. Troy was glued to me and he didn't let me out of his sight.

Carlos said, "What's up with him?"

I said, "He's scared."

"You mean the kid who couldn't wait to get into the game. The one who would do anything for money?

"Come on, Carlos. He needs us."

Carlos said, "I'm proud of you." I knew exactly what he meant. It made me feel good.

An hour later, Nick showed up and said, "What's up, boys?"

Carlos said, "Now that the work is done, you show up."

"What can I say—I've been busy."

We all went to Carlos's room to hang out until our presence was required. Carlos and Nick argued over what music to listen to.

I said, "Troy, are you okay?"

He smiled and took a deep breath. "Yes."

We were summoned for the party to begin. We all got undressed and raced out to the pool. If the guys were hoping for a show, they were going to have to look fast. We were running as fast as we could. I was last, but hot on their heels when a big, hairy guy named Bruce reached out and grabbed me, swung me around, and held me to his chest.

Nobody said anything because he was so big and strong. I tried escaping, but I couldn't get away. The more I moved and squirmed, the more he liked it. He carried me to a bedroom and there were two other guys waiting for us. It was a complete shock to me.

In two years, nothing like this had happened at a party. I wondered why it was only me they wanted. The big guy put me down once we got in the room. He blocked the door so I couldn't get out. I didn't know this was allowed and I had never heard the other kids talk about anything like this. I knew they all had seen what had happened and I was waiting for someone to rescue me. I knew Brian and Roger would come in and stop them.

As the men came closer to me and I realized there was no escaping, my mind went into panic mode. It didn't take long until my mind completely shut down. Each man had sex with me—and every one of them had fun making it painful.

When they were done, they left the room. I just lay there on the bed lifeless and curled up in a ball, waiting for the pain to go away. It hurt too much to even walk out of the room. I closed my eyes and heard the door open. I was too afraid to open my eyes. I expected the worse. I didn't dare open my eyes to find out what man was standing over me. I felt someone sit on the bed, but it was too light to be a grown man.

Troy said, "Are you okay?"

I didn't move or answer him. He pulled a blanket over my cold, naked body. I didn't say the words, but he knew how thankful I was. He comforted me and I could tell he was still wet from the pool. He had come in as soon as he knew the guys were gone.

Carlos and Nick came in and sat on the bed.

Carlos asked, "Are you all right?"

Nick said, "Good God, Timmy, suck it up. What did you think would happen to you when you came today?" *That's Nick for you, nothing gets to him.*

Carlos said, "You coldhearted bastard!"

This made us all laugh. They helped me get up and we all walked to the pool. They walked slowly because I did. The men were playing volleyball in the pool and someone had already started cooking. They stopped and stared when they saw us and started clapping for me as if I had won a race or something.

Carlos picked me up and walked me to the pool. They divided us into two teams and started playing volleyball. We only played one game before it was time to eat. The food smelled good, but my stomach was too upset to eat. Carlos and Nick were devouring their food like someone was going to steal it from them. Troy was picking at his because he was so tense. I asked Troy what was wrong, but he wouldn't answer.

Richard was keeping a close eye on Troy. He walked over, gave him a pill, and said, "That will help you."

He swallowed the pill. I didn't have the guts to ask for one, but

I really wanted one. After our normal pep talk from Carlos, we went back in the pool because the men weren't done eating. The air was cold, but the water was nice and warm. I could see the heat coming off the Jacuzzi so I went in there. I got in slow to get used to the temperature. Troy saw me and jumped in like it wasn't even hot. He was playful and loud and acted like he didn't have a care in the world. I didn't know what Richard had given him, but it wasn't a Valium.

"Troy, are you all right?

"I feel great!" *Yeah, a little too great.* He started walking around the Jacuzzi faster and faster to make a whirlpool. I put my feet up and watched him go in circles.

"Come on, Timmy. Help me." To make him happy, I walked in circles with him.

Carlos and Nick joined us and Nick asked, "What are you idiots doing?"

Troy laughed and I shrugged. They both got in.

Nick yelled, "Stop it!"

Troy yelled, "Make me!"

Carlos said, "Really, Troy, stop it."

Troy said, "No, you make me!"

Nick and Carlos reached out to grab Troy.

I said, "No. Don't! There's something wrong with him."

Nick said, "Nothing a good ass-whipping can't fix."

I said, "No really. His dad gave him a pill."

Carlos grabbed Troy, looked into his eyes, and said, "Yeah, he's high."

The men were ready for us and called us in. Troy had kept me so occupied I didn't even have time to get nervous. Carlos grabbed one of Troy's arms and Nick grabbed the other and they took off toward the house. I was right behind them but with much less enthusiasm.

When we got to the house, the men divided us up. Nick and Troy went to the garage with half the men. Carlos and I went with the other half to the living room. We were glad they had teamed us together. I was pretty good at role playing and we put on quite a show. When they were done with us, they let us go.

Instead of going to the pool, we went to Carlos's room and showered. Then we talked on the bed. When Nick and Troy came in, they both looked whipped. Carlos and I laughed after they left the room. When they were done showering, we hung out in the bedroom. When the party ended and the men left, Brian came to get me. All I could think was that it had finally been my last party.

On Monday, I went to school dreading Rick and Todd's house. I wanted it over with, but time moved extremely slowly. I had too much time to think and planned all the different ways to avoid Rick. I knew Rick had the balls to show up at my house. I had also promised Troy and I couldn't do that to him. I told Brian that I had to go straight home and help pack boxes. Brian seemed sad, but didn't question my story. When I left school, I walked like I was going to my own funeral.

Rick pulled up and said, "Hey, kid. Get in." He smiled. I tried to smile back, but it didn't work. On the way to his house, I made conversation so I wouldn't think so much. I asked him all about the hospital, life in general, and anything else I could think of.

When we got to the house, Todd said, "How did it go?"

"Fine, but I couldn't shut him up."

Troy smiled at me from the couch.

I said, "Todd, can we go in the Jacuzzi?"

"God, yes! I hate dirty little boys."

We got in and Troy thanked me for coming. This guy really thought I had a choice.

Troy seemed really nervous and I said, "What kind of movie are they making?"

"Oh, Timmy, it's horrible." He started talking ninety miles an hour about all the stuff in the garage. He told me about the tie-downs, whips, and sex toys. He thought I should be shocked and then I realized he hadn't seen all the movies Rick and Todd had made. He was getting all worked up so I tried to calm him down. I felt like Carlos when he used to help me out in these situations.

Rick came over and told us they were ready. I motioned for him to talk to me and he came to the edge of the pool.

I said, "Rick, we're scared. Tell us what's going to happen."

Troy looked surprised as Rick started to explain. Even I was surprised—those guys were really sick.

They took us to the garage and they had all the same equipment but had added a winch that hung from the rafters. They told us to fix our hair and then we would begin acting out our parts. It surprised me how good Troy was.

In one scene, Troy buckled my ankles to a rod that hooked to the winch. It pulled me up, hanging me upside down. Troy picked up a whip and started to work me over. The whip was made of soft material and didn't hurt. I acted like I was in horrible pain and put on a really good show. My head was starting to hurt from being upside down and they finally lowered me. We followed the rest of their script and then we were done.

Troy and I ran back to the pool to clean off and then swam back to the Jacuzzi. Troy was in a great mood and told me how much easier it was because I was there. I smiled at him. He was so happy it blew me away.

Rick told Troy that his dad was here to pick him up. Troy thanked me again and left. I enjoyed the heat from the Jacuzzi and closed my eyes. I smiled, knowing I didn't have much longer. I was so glad that this part of my life was coming to an end. My smile faded when I thought about Brian being out of my life too.

Rick yelled for me to come inside. I figure he was ready to take me home and I started to go get my clothes.

"What are you doing?"

"Getting dressed."

"Not yet, Timmy. Todd and I need you just a little longer."

"Why would you want me when you can have Troy?"

They both start laughing.

Rick said, "You're kidding, right?"

Todd patted me on the shoulder and said, "Timmy, you're still everyone's favorite—whether you like it or not."

I followed them into the garage. Rick drove me home later and I was so glad I had made it through my last evening with them and still had some sanity.

CHAPTER SIXTEEN

SAYING GOOD-BYE

There was very little time left before we were to move. I spent every spare minute with Brian that I could. I didn't know how I was going to live without him. He had done so much for me. He had greatly influenced me in the time I was in his life. And that time was quickly coming to an end. I would have to go on without him. The rest of my life was up to me. The choice of who I wanted to be. The choice of who I would hang out with. My future was mine for the first time in two years. I would also know what kind of adults to avoid in the future.

While walking to Brian's house for the last time, I thought back on the past two years. There were many highlights—some were extremely painful and others extremely sweet. I knew Brian was responsible for both of them. I loved him, but at times I had even hated him.

I didn't have long because Mom expected me back right away. He was on the couch preparing for his good-bye. I ran to him and hugged his neck tight and started crying. He didn't hold back either. After a few minutes, he put his hands on my shoulders and stood me in front of him.

"I'm going to explain to you why I won't be calling or coming by anymore." This was what I didn't want to hear, but it didn't totally surprise me either. "Timmy, you've got to listen to me. The group doesn't want you to go; you were too popular with them. I don't want them knowing where you are living. Some things happened to you that I didn't want and I'm sorry. You've got to know no one will ever replace you in my heart. I have loved you like a son. And remember everything we've done has to stay our secret. Okay?"

I looked him in the eye and stood up tall and strong. I said, "I'm really going to miss you. But always remember, I'm good at keeping secrets."

With that said, I turned and walked out the door.

Epilogue

When we moved to Yorba Linda, my mother's anger and rage continued. It would be many years before I would be old enough and big enough to stand up to her. Brian broke another promise and found it impossible to let me go, but that's in my book of untold stories.

When I became a man, I closed that chapter in my life—never to return to it. I became a successful businessman with a family. I had put it so far away that it would be decades before I thought about it again in detail. I always had nightmares and bad dreams; insomnia was a way of life for me. Little did I know that the whole time my mind was feeding me bits and pieces until I couldn't handle it anymore and had to face this traumatic time in my life—once and for all.

As the reality began to unfold about these horrific childhood experiences, I sought counseling. I knew I couldn't get through this madness on my own. My counselor advised me to write down the events to help clear them from my mind. My counselor read what I had written and told me he had learned a lot about child abuse—and how a child could get sucked into the dark world of child porn and keep such horrific secrets.

If you don't love a child, someone else will. If you're not watching your child, others might! It might be a predator. Our children are our most treasured asset. We would never take a diamond off and put it in the front yard and hope for the best. We treasure it and keep it on our finger or in a safe place. We don't even like to loan out something so precious and valuable. Unless we know and trust a person completely, how much more should we value our children?